The Gorga Guide to Success

Business, Marriage, and Life Lessons from a Real Estate Mogul

By Joe Gorga

with Kristen McGuiness

LIGHT HUSTLE™
PUBLISHING

ISBN-13: 978-1-7325008-6-0

Dedication

To la mia famiglia.

Table of Contents

Foreword
by Tiki Barber

The first time I met Joey Gorga, I didn't know what to expect. I only knew him as the brash Italian on *The Real Housewives of New Jersey*, and though my wife immediately liked Melissa, I wasn't sure if the feeling would be mutual with her husband. But the minute he shook my hand, I realized the show was just one part of who this guy was.

I meet a lot of celebrities – people whose fame has changed them from being normal, everyday people into divas overnight – but Joey Gorga has never lost his realness. He is the same guy he was before the show brought him and Melissa unexpected stardom: hard-working, humble, successful, and fun. And it doesn't hurt that he's a Giants fan.

The first few times I met Joey, we didn't talk about what he did for a living because he knows that before you can build a professional relationship, you need to build a personal one. Instead, we just got to know one another. We talked about football (of course!) and family. We talked about marriage and life, and by the end of that first dinner, I understood why my wife had wanted us to get to know them. They were real people; not just reality stars.

And as I got to know Joey, I found out he was a star in his own right – developing and selling properties throughout New Jersey. Because of the show, Joey spends his life "being on." And "being on" can be exhausting. It's like the radio. When that "On Air" light is lit, you're working. And so most of the time, Joey is always working. But that's the thing about Joey: he has learned to balance "being on" with being real. Whether he's at the grocery store or the mall or in the middle of a business deal, he has mastered being on a hit reality show with being a regular guy out there in the world, all while running a successful business. And he's figured out the key to that success is how he treats other people.

Joey knows how to negotiate the world of real estate because he understands that business is all about building real relationships. Whether it's overcoming the challenges of construction or thinking about how he was portrayed on last week's show, he is always focused on how to leverage relationships to create opportunity. From the minute I met Joey, it was like I had known him forever. There is a sweetness in him you just can't fake. Joey knows when to be vulnerable and when to be tough. He knows that being nice isn't just the right way to be; it's the best way to build and maintain lasting relationships.

I've been in the northeast long enough to know Italian life, and I'm honored to say my wife and I (along with our kids) have been pulled into the Gorga family. And once you get into an Italian family, you can never get out (*The Godfather* was right!). That's the thing about Italians: once they accept you, they accept you for who you really are, which is what made us feel right at home with the Gorgas. Joey and Melissa have no facade. They don't sugarcoat anything, and they love each other for it.

One of the first times we got together, my wife and I showed up in our Acadia. Because we have six kids, we need a big car. Five minutes later, Melissa and Joey showed up in a Bentley.

I turned to my wife, and was like, "So that's how they roll!"

But once they got out, Melissa and Joey were the regular couple we have come to know and love. The same ones who can get in a fight at dinner and still love each other at the end. The same ones who have incredibly busy lives but still show up for their children.

Success can take you away from your family. It's easy to get so caught up in your own goals that you ignore the people you love at home. But that is the one thing that has always impressed me with Joey and Melissa. As much as their stars have climbed, they have taken their kids along with them. They protect them from the worst of fame, but they also include them. Their #1 priority is their children, and you see that in every choice they make.

One of my brother's old coaches used to say before every game, "Gentlemen, I need some genuine enthusiasm from you today, and if you don't got it, fake it."

Joey doesn't have to fake it. Whether he's going to work, watching a game, or hanging out at the bar, Joey is enthusiastic about everything. It is what has made him such a success on the show and in real life. He brings his enthusiasm to work every day and his appreciation for life is a reminder to us all that we have to be grateful for the opportunities in our lives. His life lessons aren't just about business, and they're not just about marriage. They are touchdown truths about how to love life and create success wherever you go.

And those are two things the real Joey Gorga knows how to do.

Introduction

I never really thought I'd be the type of guy to write a book. But I also never thought I would be the type of guy to be on reality TV.

Even though a lot has changed in my life, I still think of myself as a poor Italian kid from the inner city of Paterson, NJ.

Sure, I was raised by my dad to be a good guy, to work hard, to become successful, but never in a million years did I plan to be famous.

And being famous can be a good thing or a not so good thing.

Depends on the day. And depends on how you handle it.

For me, I handle fame by sticking with my work.

I get up every morning and I go to the same job I've had for almost twenty years – developing real estate throughout New Jersey.

Some days I'm meeting with real estate agents to see what's on the market to buy, some days I'm meeting with attorneys to negotiate the deal, and some days I'm in with my guys trying to figure out what's wrong some damn sewer line.

Sure, my wife Melissa and I might be stars on *The Real Housewives of New Jersey*, but we're also real people like you.

And I'm really real, like so real.

I say it how I mean it. Because even though Melissa and I have built up a successful life together, like I said, I'm still just a poor Italian kid from the inner city of Paterson.

I'm still and will always be Joey Gorga.

Which is why when I decided to write a book, I decided it should be about the one thing I know a lot about: being a Gorga.

The Gorga Guide to Success is really just some simple rules about how to be successful in business, in marriage, and in life.

I learned most of these rules from my hard-working Italian father who not only gave my sister Teresa and I a very serious work ethic but also taught us how to be good people along the way.

Now some of you reading this might be *Housewives* fans, and others of you might be interested in becoming successful in business. Either way, I'll think you'll be surprised to find out what I've got to say about the rules to real estate.

Because over our nine seasons on *Real Housewives*, I've learned what it's like to keep my business successful while still making time for the show. Whether that means I gotta "Always Be a Magician" or "Never Turn Down an Opportunity," living in the spotlight has taught me a lot about the good and bad of business and of life.

Then there's my marriage. I think if you're married, it doesn't really matter why you're reading this book because you're gonna find out what it takes to keep the fires going, even when there are temptations all around you.

Melissa and I, we've been best friends since we first got together, but being on TV can make it hard. I mean, all marriages are hard, right? But they're really hard when everyone's watching you.

But we haven't forgotten about who we are, where we came from, or why we're together, and we've held on to all those life lessons that make us Italian and from New Jersey.

I think it doesn't matter who you are or how you know me. *The Gorga Guide to Success* can help you figure out everything from real estate deals to relationships…and how to make your dreams come true.

Just like I have.

The thing is, I didn't have any other choice in life. I didn't have a trust fund. No one in my family owned a business. I didn't have anyone to go to who would help me out.

All I had was me.

And I knew I wanted it to be more than me. I wanted to have a wife and a family, and I didn't want that family to go through what I went through.

I wanted them to have everything I didn't have.

So I went out there, and I built the kind of life I wanted – not just for myself but for my kids. And I kept on pushing until I got it.

What I've realized is that some people have that drive and some don't. But if you have it, and I'm guessing you do if you're reading this book, then you gotta make sure you play the game right, if you want to win.

The truth is no one is going to do it for you. People don't care about other people. They barely care about themselves, so you gotta get out and fight to make it happen.

Growing up, I played football, and when I was on the field, if you hit me, I was gonna come back at you twice as hard. It's been the same way in work. The harder the job, the more I keep going, even when it hurts my body. Nothing stops me. Because the more I'm getting beat up, the better I get.

That's how we learn in life – not from the easy stuff but from the stuff that beats us up. Which is why we gotta learn quick.

For me, it's the lessons that I learned as a kid that have kept me moving, have kept driving me forward. It's those life lessons that have made me successful in real estate, in marriage, and in life.

And now I'm gonna get to share them with you.

Like I said, I never thought I'd be the kind of guy who would write a book. But I got a lot to say, so let's get started.

CHAPTER 1

You Gotta Have Balls

You gotta have balls.

Most people would say you shouldn't start a book in this day and age telling people they gotta have balls, but I come the streets of New Jersey, where we say it like it is - even if other people don't like it.

See, the way I look at it, life is all about moments. Every day, you have the chance to make the most of those moments or they're just going to pass you by.

I've been successful not because I got lucky (though we all need a little luck), but because when I want something, I go for it. I risk it all and I'm not afraid to screw up. That's having balls. Being willing to be hurt. And still going ahead with the plan.

Years ago, I went after my first big real estate venture. This was before my wife Melissa and I ended up on *The Real Housewives of New Jersey*. This was before Melissa was even my wife.

I had been doing real estate deals in New Jersey for a couple of years – flipping houses, renovating old units, even running a few income properties – but then a customer reached out to me about an old mill building that he was selling in Paterson. The guy wasn't looking to close on it for another year but was interested in locking in a buyer.

"You interested?" he asked.

It was huge and falling down. Anyone I took to the property would say to me, "Joey, you're freaking out of your mind!"

But I saw something else. I saw 63 apartments and a boost to the neighborhood where I grew up.

I was raised by two hard knuckle Italian parents who came to America with barely a cent to their name, but they came with a dream like so many others before and after them. They believed that hard work and a lot of hustle would give them a better life than they had in Italy. And they taught me an important Italian lesson: "Prendere la palla al balzo." You need to take the ball at the bounce.

If we wanted to survive, we couldn't sit around waiting for the perfect deal. There are no perfect deals when you're poor with two kids living on the wrong side of the New Jersey tracks. My parents had to run for every ball that came their way, and they taught me how to run with them. So when I saw the old mill building, I knew I had to grab the ball.

I hardly had any money, but I negotiated a deal where I put in labor for the cost of the deposit, laying the foundation of the building in order to get the permits to build. I had a year to close with the down payment, which I attached to my house in case I couldn't come up with the money.

It was a huge gamble, but no one wins big at the casino by playing the penny slots.

I knew if I pulled it off, it would change my life.

After a few months, we got the foundation laid, the designs were complete, and we went before the town to present the project.

Now let me back up a second here and tell you another story.

A few months before, I was in Mexico with friends. We were at the hotel when I saw this girl walk out to the pool. She was wearing a leopard bikini and she was gorgeous. But before I could meet her, she went back to her room.

So I go over and meet her friends instead. I find out they were all from New Jersey and they tell me their friend's name is Melissa, but for the rest of the trip, Melissa and I, we keep missing each other. We all leave Mexico, but I stay in touch with Melissa's crew. I would meet up with them down at the Jersey Shore. Melissa would be there, but we still didn't connect. Sometimes I was with another girl, sometimes she was with her friends, sometimes, I would just watch her but something in me said, "Not yet."

Until that night after the meeting at the apartment building. After we presented the project to the Board, and they told us we were approved to turn that broken-down mill into rental apartments, my architect, attorney, and I decided to go out and celebrate. We headed to a place in Clifton, NJ called Joey's, which is what most people call me, so it fit.

When we walked into Joey's, guess who was there behind the bar? The girl in the leopard bikini. Melissa.

Like I said, it's all about moments. I was having the best night of my life, and I knew the minute I saw her bartending at that restaurant, that she was going to be my wife.

Just like I knew that old mill was going to become an apartment building. Just like I knew I was going to be successful.

If anyone had asked me when I was a kid what I wanted to be, that's what I would have told them. I didn't want to be a fireman or a cop. I didn't want to be president.

I wanted to be rich. And not rich for the money. I wanted to be able to run things and make my own schedule and have enough money to treat my wife like a queen and take care of my kids. My dad worked his butt off, but we were always worried about him.

We were a very tight family. My father worked hard and long hours and he trained us to work hard. He wanted us to go to school to get an education, but we could always feel that our parents were worried about money.

So we were always worried about money. We didn't spend it - we saved it, and whenever we made money, we always gave some to the household, even as kids.

Because my sister Teresa and I, we've been working since we were kids.

And what I realized was that I could let someone else take the ball or I could grab it myself. I could flip burgers for the rest of my life or I could own the restaurant. Teresa and I, we wanted to own the restaurant (more on that later).

But you don't own anything by playing it safe. I didn't have a trust fund to start investing in properties. I had to work hard, and I had to do crazy things, like buy an old mill that was falling down. I had to grab the ball on the first bounce, and I had to have the balls to do it.

So that's what I did that night, when I walked up to the bar, introduced myself to the future Melissa Gorga, and told her she was going to be my wife.

Since then, we have watched our lives explode. From that first apartment building to *The Real Housewives of New Jersey*, we built ourselves a little empire – made up of our businesses, but also of our families. And that hasn't always been easy. We've had to figure out how to be famous and still raise our kids and run a business and pick up the dry cleaning and get along with our family...and all the stuff that we did before there were cameras in our living room.

We had to figure out how to stay real after becoming famous.

And I had to find real balls. The kind that let me support my wife even when I wasn't sure I wanted to do the show. The kind that helped me negotiate tough business deals. The kind you need when you're sitting there holding your dying mom, and you got to go tell your pop that she's gone.

And no matter how long I've been married, I still gotta come home to my wife and love her with the same passion I did that first night at the bar when I was determined I was going to make her mine. I got to bring that same passion into our bedroom and that same passion into my job. And passion takes balls.

Passion means I'm willing to give my all even if it doesn't work out. Even if the economy falls apart, or the building can't get built, or that girl at the bar says "no," which Melissa did the first couple of times I asked her out.

Having balls means you don't ever quit when you know something is supposed to happen. And in real estate, the easiest thing to do is quit.

I've learned the hard way my whole life, but the hard way teaches you a whole lot more than the easy way. I had to go through some rough times to get to the good ones. There were times I didn't think that apartment building was going to happen. The same for a lot of other deals. There were times when I thought I might lose my house because of it. There were times when I thought I might lose my wife. And yeah, sure, there were times where I sat crying in my car, wondering if I was going to make it.

But I stuck it out. And in the end, it was just the beginning.

The hard way teaches you the right way to do things. It shows you how to show up for the people you love and the people you work with. It shows you how to grab the ball at the first bounce because you might not get another chance.

So life. And moments. That's why when we joined *The Real Housewives of New Jersey*, I knew it was exciting and crazy and would bring us all these opportunities, but really, it's just one moment. Melissa and I were here before it began, and we'll be here when it's over. Which is why we can't go become other people in this moment. We have to stick to who we always were, and who we'll always be.

Because every moment, we get to decide whether our choices will make us successful or not. After the first night that Melissa and I finally hung out, we started talking every day. We became friends. We got married and our lives have been filled with amazing moments ever since: our kids being born, summers at the shore, Christmas in New York City, traveling the world together, our kids' games, and being on the show.

We've made a life that's so big and full, it's just awesome. But it didn't come from nothing. I started building it when I was nine years old. I worked my ass off to get it. And I know that every day I wake up, I got to put my pants on and go out and do it again.

I got to work on my business. I got to work on my marriage.

I gotta have balls every day, in everything I do.

And you do too.

CHAPTER 2

Know How to Work

A lot of people work hard, but that's the problem. We work so hard that we forget to work smart.

For a lot of my life, I worked hard. Ridiculously hard. My parents came to the States in the early 1970s, but the way they raised us, it might as well have been the 1920s. Even now when I see old immigrant movies like *A Bronx Tale*, it looks more like my childhood than *The Brady Brunch* ever did. I didn't grow up in the Brady Bunch. We didn't have nice things or go on family vacations to Hawaii.

My father believed that work was the only thing that mattered. In order to survive, we had to work.

He and my mother came here with nothing but a dream that they could do better in America. They left behind their families, their culture, and their language with the promise that they would be able to give their kids better lives in America.

And they weren't wrong.

My father started as a mason, but after a few years he got into shoe repair, opening a small store in Paterson. Because he didn't make enough doing that, he also got a newspaper route, which in those days was like driving Uber. People did it on the side because they could start early before their real jobs and make a little extra.

His route was for over 1,000 newspapers, but he didn't have any trouble making it because he had two employees right there in his house: my sister and me. And we were free labor.

We didn't even question why we were working. I was nine years old and I would wake up at 4:00 in the morning to sling newspapers from my bicycle. Teresa would be on her bike and after we made it to the end of the block, we would go off in opposite directions in the dark, just to help our father. Because that is what you did.

I think we both knew from a young age that money was an issue. That we were poor, and unless we worked hard, we would always be poor.

And Teresa and I, we didn't want to be poor.

So we got up before the sun and we threw newspapers into our neighbors' yards, and then we would come home and eat breakfast, trying to warm up before we walked to school.

That was the other thing that my dad and mom cared a lot about: school.

They always reminded us that they came to America so we could get an education, go to college, and be somebody - people who didn't have to get their kids up at 4 in the morning, for example.

When I was 10, I got my own real job working at Rascal's Hot Dog House, making hot dogs in the back kitchen. I guess this was before child labor laws because I can't even imagine my 10-year-old making a hot dog in our kitchen, but there I was, wearing my little hat, working as soon as I got out of school until 11 o'clock at night.

So my day would start at four in the morning and it would go until 10 at night, and that was my childhood.

Which means I didn't have much of one.

But since I grew up in the rough part of Paterson, that was probably for the better.

Kids all around me were getting into trouble. They were using drugs by the time they were 10, they were selling drugs by the time they were 12, and I knew kids who were already going to prison (not even juvie) by the time I was in high school.

All around me I saw what being poor could do to you, and I didn't want any of it. This was the 1980s and all you had to do was look at your friend's MTV (because there was no way my dad was paying for cable) to see what the world had to offer: fancy cars and pretty girls, big mansions and those swimming pools with the hot tub attached.

I wanted one of those pools. But more than anything, I wanted to stop worrying about how hard my dad worked just to put food on the table.

So it wasn't just that I had to help my dad; I wanted to.

On the weekends, I would help him with our yard. It was just 14 square feet of grass, but I would still pull the weeds and push the mower while my other friends rode by on their bikes. While they were off having fun, I would be on my knees next to my dad, in our garden, pulling tomatoes.

Because that was the other hard rule about growing up Italian: family was everything.

I loved my friends (and still do), but my parents and my sister were my world.

Teresa and I both lived in fear of my dad. He never once touched us, and yet it was as though we thought the guy might kill us - that old "I brought you to this world and I can take you out of it" thing.

I remember when I was about eight, my sister and I were messing around in the bathroom and we got water everywhere. My dad came in to yell at us and my sister got so freaked out she ran right into the doorknob. She got a black eye…from herself. I wish my kids feared me one tenth as much.

The Mexicans have a saying: "Mucho trabajo poco deniro." Too much work for a little bit of money. That was our childhood.

My father worked from sunrise to sundown just so we could survive. But I wanted to do more than survive.

There was never a time in my childhood when I wasn't working, and it was the same when I was a teenager. I was either at a job, in school, or on a football field (more on that later). And when I got to college, it was no different. I played college ball all while running my own landscaping business. The thing was, I knew I wasn't going to be a professional football player, and I could see that the landscaping business could make me a lot of money. And college costed me a lot of money.

Though I want my kids to go to college, I knew that I didn't need a degree to become successful. I just had to work hard.

But as I was quickly learning, I also needed to learn how to work smart.

There's an Italian saying: "Braccia rubate all'agricoltura." It means: you're only smart enough to work on the farm.

I didn't want to spend my life working the farm. I wanted to grab that ball on its first bounce, so instead, I went from doing some landscaping on the side to launching my own landscaping business.

I was living with my parents - like most good Italian boys - and I started marketing myself to all the neighbors. I made up these little flyers and rode my bike to the nicer neighborhoods like I did when I had the paper route, stuffing them in all the mailboxes. I would go to the mall and put those flyers on everyone's cars. Everywhere I went, I left my flyers. All I had was my bike, the Nissan, and my dad's rusty lawnmower, but I figured that was enough.

If I was lucky enough to run into the residents of the neighborhood, I would tell them that I would do the job for $5 less that their current guy. Not everyone said yes - but some did, and I started getting more clients and taking care of bigger yards in richer areas.

One of my first big jobs was for a rich guy in Franklin Lakes. The guy drove a Mercedes, which to me made him seem like Donald Trump.

The first day I got to his house, I went out in the front yard and began mowing it like a square - just like I did in my dad's yard since all he had was 15 square feet of grass. This guy came out his front door and yelled at me, "What are you doing? Haven't you ever mowed a yard before?"

I stopped in my tracks. "You got to do it in a circle," he said, motioning with his hands. "I want it in a circle."

So I did it in a circle, and the next week, when the guy asked me if I could build a wall, I said sure - but I knew this time, I'd better figure out what I was doing before I got there.

That week, I went to the library (this was back before Google) and read up on how to build a wall. To practice, I even I built a wall in my dad's backyard. I finally went the next week and built a wall around part of the guy's garden, and I did such a good job, he had no idea I'd been lying through my teeth the week before.

Every time I would do something new, I would add it to my little flyer. So now I didn't just do land-scaping - I did construction too.

I took the work ethic my dad taught me and I started putting it to use.

A guy I had worked for in college offered to sell me some of his landscaping customers. Basically, for $15,000, he would sell me 30 of his customers. The only thing was they were about 10 miles from my house.

With all these new clients, I knew it was time to get my own equipment, but I had no credit. I was just a college dropout mowing people's lawns with a 10-year-old mower. But my sister Teresa had started working and she had credit cards. These days, every-one uses credit cards to buy things they can't afford, but back then, we used them to buy things that could help us make money so we could afford to buy things.

I maxed out her two cards for a sit-down mower and all the tools I would need to start really working on people's yards. I mean, none of it was nice. It was like *Sanford & Sons* - junkyard equipment. But it was mine, and I was determined those first 30 clients were going to bring me 30 more.

Unfortunately, the night before my first day in the neighborhood, my truck broke down.

I called up the friend who was going to help me on the houses and the next morning, we left my house on the riding lawnmower, driving the thing 10 miles across town. My friend hung off the back, holding a garbage can filled with all the tools I had just bought.

I found a safe place where I could keep the mower and my tools, and every day, my friend and I would walk the 10 miles to get there and back.

After the first month, I got together enough money to fix my truck and didn't have to use my mower like a car anymore. But I learned that if you want to make a business work, you have to be willing to work it.

Over the next few years, I would grow the landscaping business before I started moving into construction and then real estate. With every move, I learned that while working hard gets you in the door, working smart takes you up the elevator.

Over the next two decades, I decided I was tired of lugging equipment 10 miles on a sit-down mower. I wanted to zip across town in a Bentley.

And not because being rich meant I was better than anyone else, but because I'd worked hard enough for long enough to know that there had to be a better way.

I wanted to own a beautiful home and not worry every month about how I was going to pay for it. I wanted to spoil my wife so she knew there was no one else on the planet who was going to treat her as good as I could. And I wanted to make sure my children had everything they needed without having to wake up at four in the morning to throw newspapers off the back of their bikes.

But if they did need to toss papers, I knew I wanted them to do it with a smile.

Because that is also what my dad taught us: that you shouldn't go to work with a frown on your face. There are a lot of people in this world who would kill to have your job, even if you have the worst job in the world. There is someone out there with no job at all.

Work is a privilege and you should do it with a smile.

That's why in those early days of landscaping, I got the routes. I got the clients. I got the opportunities. Because I went out there every day on my rickety lawnmower with a smile on my face. I asked how people were doing. I enjoyed my job even when it was hard, or exhausting, or I was driving a lawnmower across town. I made work fun even when it was heartbreaking, and still do to this day. Even when it's tough shooting *Housewives*, I still try to remember all the benefits that come with opening my life for the show.

A few years ago, my wife and I were at a press event for the show with some other reality stars from another franchise. I was talking to fans and taking pictures and one of the other stars turned to Melissa, and said, "Wow, he really loves this."

The thing is I don't always love it. It can be exhausting. But I appreciate it and try to enjoy it.

Because it isn't just about working hard or working smart...it's about working happy.

And if you go to work happy, you will always enjoy your work. But even more importantly, people will enjoy working with you. They will want to hire you. They will want to do right by you. There will always be jerks out there looking to screw you over, but if you're not one of those jerks, you're won't have to tangle with the bad guys as much.

Growing up, I knew if I didn't make it, no one else was gonna do it for me. I didn't have a choice but to work hard.

But I also knew I didn't want to always be out in the fields. Though I'll still get in the dirt with my guys any day of the week, I wanted more than that. I didn't want to work in the kitchen, I wanted to be the boss.

I wanted to run my own thing. I wanted to run my own empire.

Whether you're tossing papers or flipping houses, only you can determine how successful you can be. Work hard, work smart, work happy.

And it'll feel like you've never worked a day in your life.

CHAPTER 3

Never Turn Down Opportunity

When I was 11, I decided I wanted to play sports. The only problem was there was no way my dad was going to let me. He believed that unless you were going to become a professional athlete, it was more important that you spent your time working. And you were never going to become a professional athlete.

But I disagreed.

So I tried out for the football team, and I made it. I decided that with my work schedule, I would be able to keep my new hobby away from my dad. It was simple. I would go to work from 3-6 pm at the hot dog shack, take a break from work from 6:30-8:00 (which they let me do), and then go back to work at 8:30 until we closed at 10:30. I would head home and shower after my dad was in bed and no one needed to know a thing.

Of course, my mom knew because moms always know. She would wait up for me every night with a warm meal so I could eat before bed and would see the big bag of football equipment I tried to sneak in the house every night. Instead of telling my dad though, she just started washing my gear in secret so that every day, I had a clean uniform at practice (I was the only one on the team with clean clothes – but then again, I was also the only Italian).

I didn't want to lie to my dad, but I also knew that I couldn't pass up the opportunity to play. From my first tryout, it was obvious to everyone - including me - that I knew how to play ball.

I was a fast runner and quick with the plays. By the third practice, I was already looking like one of the best players on the team. Now, I could have said sorry, I can't do this, but I had to take a chance at something I loved.

Business is all about risk. And in real estate, every venture is a risk. There are a million people telling you no, telling you that you can't do this or that. There are a million reasons not to buy the house, invest in the property and try to turn a profit, but you can't get caught up in someone else's "no." You gotta say "yes" when the opportunity comes up.

Even when it means you're going to have to work extra hard to make it happen.

Which is what I did for those first weeks of playing football behind my dad's back. Practice was going along fine - but then the games began. The games were scheduled for Sunday afternoons, which would have been fine if I'd been part of a different family. For Italian families, Sunday afternoons are sacred. We had Sunday dinner every weekend, which started at 2:00 pm. And the one cardinal rule of Sunday dinner was that you could not be late. Since the games began at 1:00 pm, I was going to be late.

I told my dad that I had to work, that the Rascal House was paying me time-and-a-half for Sundays and that I needed the money. I was only 12 years old, so I don't know what I would have needed the money for. Obviously, my father didn't really buy the story either, but he let me go on acting like I was heading to work when I was really headed to the game.

I made it to three games before I was out there on the field one Sunday afternoon. It was a great game. I was making all the plays and scored a touchdown, showing everyone that this scrawny Italian belonged on the team.

Around halftime, I'm taking a water break and I look over into the stands and who's sitting there but my father. So now I'm shitting my pants - what's he going to do when the game is over? But I just keep playing, doing my best out there on the field.

I ended up scoring six touchdowns that game. Afterwards, everyone's running up to my father – the coaches, other players, some teachers – telling him what a great player I am. They have no clue that this is the first time he has seen me play and that up until today, he wasn't even sure I was playing.

But then I see the expression on his face and I know he isn't angry at me. He's proud.

I go up to him after and he tells me, "I don't like that you lied to me, but if you're going to play that good, keep playing."

That's the thing about opportunity. If we make the most of it, all the work and shenanigans become worth it. Because if you're going to play that good, you should keep playing.

After that first Sunday, my dad made it to every game - and when I told him I wanted to play baseball, he bought me a mitt and went with me to tryouts.

He saw that I was willing to do what I needed to do to take advantage of any opportunities, which made him support me.

There's no difference when you're doing real estate. Once you can prove you know what you're doing, people will be willing to support you. They'll want to invest in your work. You'll begin to see more yes's than no's.

The game of football is all about seeing opportunities. You go out there with your play but at any minute that play might need to be changed. There could be an obstacle suddenly in your way - one of your players doesn't end up where he's supposed to be, or you make a mistake and need to do something different to fix it. You can't be afraid to look for the new opportunity at every turn.

There is a great quote that says, "The game of life is a lot like football. You have to tackle your problems, block your fears, and score your points when you get the opportunity."

I would say the same thing about the game of real estate. You can't be afraid of the problems that are going to rise in a real estate deal, because there will always be problems. Contractors won't show up, permits won't get approved, and people will screw you over.

You can be afraid to confront those problems, or you can see how to find the opportunities - even when the end zone looks blocked and there's five scary dudes between you and the touchdown.

There's an old Italian saying: "Senza tentazioni, senza onore." It basically means "no glory without temptation." You gotta want the touchdown. You gotta want the gorgeous girl or guy or whatever. You gotta want to make it so bad that you're willing to risk it all to get it.

When I was a kid, my dad was the all. We lived in fear of him, sure - but more importantly, we respected him and we wanted his respect. After that first day on the football field, my dad started to support me in sports. And later on, when I was in the Little League "World Series," he was there at the game.

Because we're Italian, my dad used to wear a lot of gold - even if you didn't have a lot of money, you always wore a lot of gold. After the game, he comes up to me and he slips the gold ring off his finger and slides it onto mine, like I had just won the real World Series.

Someone took a picture of it and it made it into the newspaper.

Here I was, this Italian kid from the inner city, playing sports for the first time in my life and killing it. Because it was the inner city, I was usually the only white kid on the team (and depending on who we were playing, the only white kid in the game). But I didn't care. I was someone who was friends with everyone, because I realized that opportunities don't just happen on the field. They happen every day through other people.

Look, you're not gonna like everyone - that's just a fact. But you gotta be nice to them. You gotta live with heart cause it's through your heart that the opportunities, they come.

Whether it was friends I met at school or people I worked with, one job would always lead to another - and then later, when I got into real estate, my customers became my references. I bought my first building from someone who had been a landscaping client. I learned about houses from agents I worked with on other properties. I became friends with the right attorneys and guys who worked in the permit offices.

Because of everyone I got to know, they had a choice: they could be the running back on my team or they could be playing for the opposing side. The opportunity eventually came when I showed them they'd do better playing for my team.

Because that was the other thing I learned from football: you can do a lot of it alone but you gotta find the right teammates.

You gotta tempt people to your side. You gotta show them that they're gonna win that World Series if you join their team, and you gotta slide that ring on their finger when you win together. You gotta reward people for helping you score the opportunity because that's how they'll come back and help you again.

My good friend Tiki Barber talks about this in his own book. He writes about how a play works out on the football field, how the entire team has to come together to make a touchdown happen.

Sure, in the end, it was Tiki landing the ball and blowing a kiss to his fans, but there were 10 other guys on the field who helped him get there.

When I was out there on the field, I felt like I had another Italian family, people I could trust (heck, sometimes, even more than my own family) and who had my back because I had theirs. Once I got into real estate, I realized the game was no different.

You can't have two quarterbacks on the field together. So me, I'm the builder - I don't need to partner with another builder. I need the money - the person who wants to sit in the office and bankroll the thing - while I'm out there at the site.

Those are the partnerships that work.

You get two developers together and then everyone's ego gets all up in the business.

But you also need to play at your level. You can't jump on the varsity team when you're still JV.

Years ago, this billionaire developer reached out to me (no, not Trump). He had seen one of my apartment buildings and he liked the look.

He invited me to his office in Manhattan and he pulled out this binder of properties he owned, filled with hundreds of buildings and houses - commercial, residential, you name it.

He asks me what I would do with them. This guy wines and dines me, takes me out to $5,000 dinners, shows me the good life. And then he asks if I want to go into business together: he buys the properties and I develop them.

I'm thinking, "This is amazing. This guy is gonna change my life."

Then I get the contract, and in it, the guy wants me to put the three apartment buildings I owned into his pool, and I'm thinking why does he want my buildings? This guy has hundreds of buildings and now he wants mine too?

He had four lawyers working in his office and I knew right away that if I signed that contract, those lawyers would eat me alive.

I realized that there was another opportunity there. I could make it without some billionaire manipulating me. I could do it on my own.

Opportunity is doing the job even when you think you can't. But in high school, my job was to prove to my dad that I could both work and play football.

I held up my end of the deal by working every day around practice times, just like I had when I was sneaking around, and by working 50-60 hours a week in the summer during off-season.

Then I got so good at football, it looked like I might actually make a career out of it.

I went to college on a scholarship, but in my first year, I tore my ACL in practice and wasn't able to play football - so they took my scholarship away. Gone were my dreams of the NFL. It wasn't easy. I had spent almost 10 years on that big, green field. I wasn't sure what I would do next, but I knew I couldn't quit on myself. I just had to find the next opportunity.

Which is pretty much what happened when the *Housewives* franchise came our way. Melissa and I didn't even know Teresa was signed up for the show until she started shooting and word got around through my folks that she was involved in some reality show. At the time, Teresa and I had lost touch. Her life with Joe had gotten tough and like all families, we had a falling out. So we were surprised when the producers called us about the show.

My wife was excited, but I wasn't as sure. What would it do to our life? What would it do to our kids?

I knew I had built a strong business. I could either let this opportunity pass us by or I could say yes - just as I did when I was a kid and saw the sign-up sheet for football.

Melissa was way more excited than I was, but then again, she had a lot more to gain and a lot less to lose. I knew how much it meant to her, and I love my wife. I wanted her to be happy.

We met with the producers, and then it took me a whole month to decide if I wanted to do it. It was one of the worst months. I was so stressed out about it.

It might sound like an easy decision – sure, we'd have the chance to become famous and make money and always be moved to the front of the line – but what would we be giving up?

Our privacy? Our family? Our marriage?

It wasn't easy, but just like that old football quote, we decided to tackle our fears and score the points. For Melissa and me, the show has totally changed our lives. It has taken us to places we never thought we'd go. We've gotten to meet so many people from all over the world, from famous people to fans. And we've been able to create a life for our children where they'll be able to play whatever sport they want without having to work three jobs in order to stay on the team.

"Senza tentazioni, senza onore." Without tempta-tion, there's no glory. Even if there have been times when being on TV made our life and our marriage really hard, it was still all worth it. Any good oppor-tunity will do that - you have to sacrifice for success, whether you're on the football field or in your home.

Today, I am the coach of my son's football team. When I watch all those little ragazzos on the field, I know he is learning about life and work and business out there. He is learning to lead and he is learning to follow. He is learning to never turn down an oppor-tunity because when the ball comes whistling through the air, when you hear the fans screaming in the stands, you only have one choice.

Touchdown!

CHAPTER 4

Put Two Feet in One Boot

Growing up Italian, there were a lot of rules. A lot. I remember watching my other friends get away with murder (or pretty close to it) while I wasn't allowed to leave the table until my plate was clean. When you're a kid, you think your parents are just torturing you for fun. I'm pretty sure my kids think I'm having a blast grounding them, but when I started working, I learned that those life lessons made all the difference.

Especially in the world of real estate.

Those other kids who got away with murder? Well, some of them have actually been convicted of murder. Growing up in the inner city, my parents knew they had to have us on a tight leash. Danger was around every corner. And they were determined that we weren't just going to be safe, but that we were going to be given the chance to be successful.

They knew the best way to be successful was to know when it was your turn.

Because as much as you have to jump at opportunity, you also need to know your place in the world.

The one thing we realized since Melissa and I began meeting more famous people is that many of them think they're really important. They think they know everything and that everyone around them is less than them.

But my parents taught Teresa and I that we all put our pants on one leg at a time, and that we all need to "put two feet in one boot."

That was the lesson every time we went over to someone else's house. Now, back then, it really meant "don't run around the other person's house like a hooligan and break stuff." But what I know now is that putting two feet in one boot is learning how to be respectful of other people.

And if the real estate world is built on anything, it's respect.

Early on, I figured out that if I wanted to grow my business, I had to do it better, faster, and for cheaper than the next guy. I would earn the customer's respect so that the next year, I could raise the price and still hook their three best friends. I would get jobs done in three days that would take other people a week. Every dollar I made, I saved. And in my landscaping business, I took on anything that could make money. I never said no to anybody - no job was too small and no job was too big.

I paid my dues. I kept two feet in one boot, even when it would have been easier to hire other people to do the work for me. Even when I wanted to quit or just go home and sleep, I knew that if I wanted respect from my clients, I had to earn it.

People say when it comes to being successful, you need to be the first one in and the last to leave. That's what people knew me for. My father was a tough man, but he taught us that at the end of the day, no matter what you had or won or lost in life, the work would always be there.

And through the work, you earn others' respect.

Like I said: the more you hit me, the stronger I get. Work was the same way. The harder I worked, the more I wanted to work.

One day, one of my customers asked me to cut down this big tree in his backyard. This thing must have been about 35 feet tall, but the guy offered me $3,000. In those days, that was like a month's worth of work, so of course I said I could do it.

He tells me that he needs me to do it on Tuesday because he'll be home, and that I need to be really careful because he just installed this $25,000 grill in the backyard and he doesn't want anything happening to it.

I'm like, "Of course not. I'll be there on Tuesday."

I knew if I came on Tuesday, it would be a mess. The guy would be watching my every move - and I was just getting my moves down.

So instead, I arrived the Thursday before, when I normally did his yard. I went to Home Depot beforehand and bought this $39 nylon rope. A customer of mine had given me spikes to climb the tree. And one of the guys who worked with me agreed to help out from below. I was determined.

We get to the house and I manage to climb to the top of the tree. This thing is huge. It's an old oak tree and probably about three feet wide. The tree is almost touching the house. I thought I would start by trimming down the branches at the top, but once I got up there and looked down, I froze. I never knew I had a fear of heights, but sitting there at the top of that tree - with nothing holding me to it and nothing below to catch me - freaked me out.

I look down and my friend is there laughing at me.

"You ever going to come down?" he calls.

I take a deep breath and see that if I get on the roof, it will be easier to tie the rope around the tree. I call down to my buddy and tell him to bring the truck around.

I tie the rope and head back down to cut the base of the tree, tying the rope to the back of the truck. My buddy gets back in the truck and I tell him to hit the gas, thinking the tree will fall forward and we can chop it up from there.

But this is my first time cutting down a tree. And this is also my first time doing it to a 35-foot tree.

I don't know if I cut the tree wrong or if my friend accelerated too fast but all of a sudden, the tree starts falling…in the wrong direction.

I try to catch it, which is ridiculous.

All I can do is watch as it careens towards both the house and the grill.

And then lands right between them both.

My friend and I start hooting and hollering. We can't believe we've pulled it off.

We quickly chop up the tree, lining it up real nice next to the grill, and when the guy gets home, he asks me what we're doing there, but I tell him since we were already doing his yard, we decided to take out the tree.

"What?" he starts to yell, getting pissed. "I wanted you to do that on Tuesday!"

"Well, it's already done," I tell him as we walk to the backyard and he sees the tree gone and, in its place, clean rows of freshly cut wood. I knew the guy was a real neat freak so we made sure it looked great.

He nods, and starts to smile, "Nice job, boys."

From that day, I started doing trees, adding it to my flyer.

The business was continuing to grow but just as my dad showed me, with each new step, I had figure out where to take it next.

The landscaping business was great for my bank account but it was killing my body. Even though I now had guys working for me, I continued to keep two feet in one boot. I believed that work always got done better and faster if I was on the job. I'm sure my guys would have preferred it if I'd stayed home, but you don't get people's respect by calling in the work. You gotta show your face, you gotta build the relationships, and sometimes you gotta climb to the top of the tree to get the job done yourself.

My father did more than teach us when to keep our mouths shut. He also taught us when we needed to stand up for ourselves and each other.

He used to tell me, "I don't ever want you to get in a fight, but you need to protect your sister."

My sister and I grew up in a rough neighborhood where there were few white kids. Most of the kids accepted us because that's just what kids do, but as we got older, we needed to earn the respect of those who didn't. We had to show them they couldn't mess with us.

I remember when I was in fifth grade, there was this kid who liked my sister. He kept bothering her - and this was a big, tough kid. One day, we were walking home from school and he started running his mouth to her. I tried not to say anything. I knew my dad would kill me if I got in a fight, but then the guy goes and hits my sister's butt. My sister is one tough cookie, but I could see her face go red with embarrassment when he did it. And my face went red with rage.

We were walking past a house. I grabbed one of those red, oval picnic chairs and I smacked this kid with it across the back of his head. It was like something out of a wrestling match. The kids all freaked out and I ran and hid with my sister.

The next day at school I thought for sure the other kids would be out to kill me. This kid had a lot of friends, and I had just embarrassed him in front of everyone.

My sister and her older friends promised to protect me, but they didn't need to. No one messed with me or my sister after that. We earned their respect and even throughout high school, I stayed friends with everyone. Black, white, Blood, Crip, stoner, jock: I was friends with everyone in the school. People respected me because I knew when to keep my mouth shut and when to stand up and fight.

I have found that nothing will help you more in business than knowing not only when you need to keep both feet in one boot but also when you need to kick the boot off.

There are going to be times when you need to fight for what you deserve – when someone tries to rip you off or when a job is going south. But then there are times when you gotta be that kid at your parent's friend's house. When you gotta say "thank you" and "please" and be real nice.

I've learned that the one place you gotta keep your mouth shut is when you're trying to get permits. You can be a loud-mouthed jackass on any other day of the week, but when the inspector comes to your site, it is all "yes sir" and "no sir" and "yes please."

It isn't easy. A lot of the guys come in knowing they've got something over you, and you want to just grab the red picnic chair and start a fight - but that could delay your project for months and lose you millions. At first, I didn't know this. I thought I could argue with the guys. I thought I knew best.

But being right isn't going to get you a permit. Being nice will.

Now, when I work those guys, I do my best to keep my mouth shut other than to become their buddies. I don't want a pissing contest with them because I can't do anything to them, but they can definitely mess with me.

Keeping two feet in one boot is all about knowing your place and knowing who you can mess with and who you can't. Too many times we ruin a good deal because we don't play nice with the people we need to.

Or we play nice with the people we shouldn't. There is another great Italian saying that goes: "La troppa bonezza finisce nella monnezza." It basically means "being too good puts you in the trash."

Now, I have built a reputation on being a nice guy, but I also know when to pull out the can of whoopass. I'm not about violence, but you gotta be willing to stand your ground or, like that saying goes, you'll end up in the trash.

Working in the construction business in New Jersey definitely takes balls. You work with a lot of characters, guys that look like they just stepped off the set of *The Sopranos*, and the truth is, they're actually in that line of business. You don't want to be a jerk to those guys, but you also can't be a pushover. Because those guys do actually put people in the trash.

You have to be tough. And you have to get the job done.

I've worked in landscaping and waste management and construction and development and real estate and reality shows, and I can tell you: in none of those businesses does being a jerk get you to the top. But being weak doesn't take you there either.

It's all about respect. Someone once asked: "Is it better to be feared or liked? What's best is to be both."

You need people to like you in order to get the job done, but you also need them to know they can't mess with you. And if that means you need to get a little Italian from time to time, then so be it: "la troppa bonezza finisce nella monnezza."

Still, the one area where we learned to be respectful was at home. Not having a lot actually made it easier for my parents to keep us in line.

Now, my kids can have almost anything they want, and though Melissa and I work to keep them humble, the truth is they have access to way more than we ever did when we were growing up. All that stuff makes it tough for them to actually get what they deserve. Melissa and I couldn't buy respect growing up; we had to earn it. That won't always be the case with my kids, so Melissa and I have to work doubly hard for them to understand that just because they have more than other kids, that doesn't mean they shouldn't learn how to work for things.

I worked so hard as a kid that I barely had a childhood. Though I don't want that for my kids, I also want them to know when to keep both feet in one boot - even if they have a lot of boots. That's why I love that they play sports and do cheerleading and have other hobbies. They don't get an award or a win just for being there (screw those participation trophies – they go in the trash in our house); they need to work for the honor.

They need to know when to shut up and when to stand up. Our sons know they need to protect their sister, and our daughter knows that the most important thing she can protect is her reputation. After all, we can work for years earning respect from other people, but in one night, we can lose it all.

That's as true for my daughter as it is for my sons, just as it is for Melissa and me. We can't just do right today. We gotta do right every day.

I can promise you those stakes only get higher the more successful you are. We have to be so squeaky clean with our word that no one can ever mess with us. We have to earn people's respect, but we also have to keep it. We have to remember the lessons both of our fathers taught us.

Then we gotta teach them to our own children.

CHAPTER 5

The Money in the Bank Makes No Money

The landscaping business was brutal. Cutting trees was busting up my body, and the schedule almost killed me. Literally.

I would work from four in the morning until night, and then I would try to go out with friends or my girlfriend.

My friends all made fun of me because I would come home from work, jump in the shower, and then pass out in the car when they picked me up to go out.

I would sleep on our way to the club but I would wake up when we got there. I would eat and drink and dance but as soon as we got back in the car, I would pass back out on the way home so I could get up again the next morning and get back to work.

One night, I was driving home from Atlantic City. I had gotten up at four in the morning to get to work and I was so tired that I ran into a telephone pole. I would pass out at dinner. People would think I was on drugs, but I wasn't. I was just exhausted.

Though the money was good, it wasn't enough to really do something with. So I started doing other side hustles – buying dead stock from stores like Target and reselling their goods. I started going to trade shows and flipping merchandise. I started rehabbing restaurant equipment and selling that to restaurants.

I was making money but it was just money in the bank.

And money in the bank makes no money.

Through my landscaping jobs, I had started meeting more and more builders.

I could tell these guys were more than rich. They owned properties that were making them money in their sleep. They could actually sleep because they didn't have to work 20 hours a day to make a living.

The other problem with landscaping in New Jersey is that for three months, you got no work because no one's working on their yards in the middle of winter. You're losing money for an entire season. Once November rolled around, I was just hustling to survive.

I knew I needed to be doing something else and I could see that real estate might just be that thing.

I wanted to create a business I could rely on. Something that would be making me money while I continued to grow my other businesses.

So I started looking around for a good opportunity. And I found it in the same town I had grown up in: Paterson.

It was a two-family unit in a rough neighborhood. It cost me $60,000. There were crackheads and drug dealers living on the street in front of it, but I had grown up in a neighborhood just like it. The house had good bones and a price I could afford.

The only problem was I had no idea what I was doing.

The plastered walls were cracking, the wallpaper was peeling off, the paint had been caked on over the decades.

I did what I knew how to do. I went to work.

I spackled the entire house. I got a roller and put popcorn walls everywhere to cover up the cracks (luckily, rough walls were in at the time).

I sanded down the old trim and all the old lead paint covering the walls.

I showed up every day at 6:00 am and left at 6:00 pm. I ran from the house to my landscaping jobs.

I repainted and ripped out the floors and put in carpeting. I put linoleum in the kitchen. I did everything cheap but good. It looked like quality even if it was just me working alone all night. Nothing was easy. The plumber tried to take my money and not do the work and I had to get Italian with him, banging down his door in the middle of the night in order for him to take me seriously.

The house had asbestos siding on it and vines climbing up one of the exterior walls. I had to strip the whole thing down and add aluminum siding. I spray-painted the whole house grey. I did my own roof. It wasn't going to win any awards, but it worked.

When I was done, I listed it for $160,000 and I got it. I made $100,000 off that first house and it was the most money I had ever made - and the best. I'll never forget walking away with that check. I was 21 years old and I had just made $100,000 for six months of work.

That day, I was grateful my father hadn't given me a trust fund. Instead, he taught me how to be a man. How to show up every morning and figure it out. He showed me that I didn't need other people to make me successful. I just needed ambition with a shit-ton of determination.

The thing was, it didn't really matter what the number was on the check. It was just proof that I was making it as a businessman.

Money in the bank makes no money. I was now taking what I made and turning it into something way more.

You can put your money in the stock market and wait years for a return but you're always risking a bust. You can have your pension or your 401k but you can't use them whenever you want without penalty. And you can keep working 70 hours a week for some hourly wage, or you can make your first small investment in real estate and watch your world change overnight.

That same year, I got into my second flip. It wasn't as easy as the first one. There were tenants in the three-family home I bought and it was a nightmare getting them out, particularly since it was my first time trying that. But I got the house for $55,000 - even less than the first one - and I was determined to make another solid profit in the same year.

I immediately saw that this was a new way of life, and one that I could rely on.

I kept the landscaping business, even moving into some waste management, but I was always looking for the next good deal.

And what I see is that real estate is everything. Either you're making rent or you're selling properties and walking away with that big check, taking it to the bank.

I just looked at a property with three units in it. The parents who'd owned it had just passed away, leaving it to their kids. It looked like shit property, but those three kids could now make a million dollars off of it. Because real estate isn't just an investment for yourself, it's an investment for your family. It's the gift we leave to our kids when we go.

The Italians are right when they say, "I soldi non fanno la felicità" - but while money may not buy happiness, owning properties can make you sleep a lot better at night.

That is, when they're not keeping you up.

I learned right off the bat that developing real estate was way trickier than cutting down a 35-foot tree. It was like jumping through one fiery hoop after the next, and there were times when I was gonna get burned.

If I wanted to be successful in real estate, I had to keep my cool.

My father and mother never said, "I love you," but they would always tell us, "Watch your soul."

I don't even know how to spell the Italian translation, but as I started out in real estate, their words came back to me. I wasn't into it just to become a rich guy.

I wanted to actually do right by my family. I wanted to repay my dad for all his hard work, and I wanted to start a family of my own.

I wanted to make a better life not just for me, but for them.

For the first time in years I was back in Paterson, turning old, run-down houses into something the neighborhood could be proud of. I started making friends with the city planners, who wanted to see more projects like mine.

Since then, I've worked in fancy neighborhoods and tough ones. Both have their plusses and minuses, but there was no way I could have gotten my start in the fancy neighborhoods.

The rougher parts of town gave me a chance to figure out what I was doing. The neighbors didn't complain, people weren't breathing down my neck asking when things were gonna to get done, and though there could be problems when the people around were selling drugs or prostituting, most people just wanted a nice, safe place to live.

That's the other thing about real estate: we all just want a nice, safe place to live.

I saw that I was doing a lot more for people building those houses than I was mowing their yards. I was making the neighborhoods better so that people could sell their own houses for more, and that helped to make the neighborhoods safer.

Paterson still has its rough parts but it's a much better town than it was 20 years ago when I started investing in it.

In the end, real estate not only helped me make money - it helped me watch my soul. By the age of 23, I was already seeing what I could do with it.

I was on the lookout for real estate deals everywhere I went. I started learning how to do everything I could to get into the next house.

But first I wanted to get into a house that was mine.

CHAPTER 6

You Get Yourself Into Trouble, You Get Yourself Out of It

Nowadays, no one wants to own up to making a mistake. It's all "pass the buck" and "cover your ass" out there. And I gotta tell you, nowhere is this truer than in the world of real estate. It makes sense. There's always someone else to blame when you're trying to do a deal. The real estate agent blames the lawyer, the lawyer blames the developer, the developer blames the contractor, the contractor blames the inspector...you get the picture.

It's one long line of "it was the other guy."

But my dad taught us that if you made the mistake, you gotta pay for it.

Sure, it's easier and sometimes cheaper to pass it down to the next guy in line – and if it was his fault, then you better – but owning your own bad deals will always make you more successful in the end.

My father instilled the fear of God in us. I mean, growing up, I still got into trouble, just like any other Italian kid in New Jersey. I drank, I went to parties, I got into fights - but the difference was I never got caught.

I would run through sheetrock. I would leap over houses and jump seven-foot fences and I would make it home because I was that scared of getting busted by my dad. I was involved in the trouble but I always got out of it.

It's no different in business. When you see trouble, you gotta get out.

There is always going to be the deal that tempts you, that makes you think you can get away with this or that. And sometimes you can. But once you see that things are going sideways, you better start looking for a fence to jump. And if you get into trouble, you better be prepared to get yourself out.

The first home I lived in was a real trouble maker. By that point, I had already flipped two other properties, but I found this great lot in Franklin Lakes and decided I would build my own house.

Through my construction business, I met this builder named Sal who started hiring me to help with his projects. I would do the landscaping and hardscaping outside, and he'd show me a little bit about framing.

Sal was about 30 years older than me, and from where I was looking, he seemed really successful. I started paying attention to how he ran his business. He became like a mentor to me. The guy was fixing and selling around 30 properties at a time, and I was like, "Yeah, I want to do that."

I had been dating a girl since high school and was now 23. Back in my neighborhood that was when you got married, so I figured it was my turn. I was planning to propose to my high school sweetheart and decided I should buy my first house before I did.

So I find this property in Franklin Lakes, but I knew that once I put in the down payment, I wasn't going to have much left to fix it up. I told Sal about the place and he told me not to worry.

"Look," he offered. "I can help you. I got a place that could use your help, and then I can have my guys do yours."

It seemed like a fair trade. Sal connected me with his architect, helping me with the permits. We hired a foundation guy because it was more than I could pull off. By the time we were ready to start the framing, I went in and helped Sal's crew with a house they were finishing - doing the entire outdoor space, from building the retaining wall to landscaping the property.

I had been working with Sal for almost a year at that point. He was like an uncle to me – we went out to dinner, got drinks, and watched games together. And now he was walking me through building my first house from scratch. I had no reason to think he wouldn't hold up his end of our agreement.

The deal was I would just pay for the cost of his crew, who came in and framed out about half the house. Then, three weeks later, I received a bill from Sal.

It was for way more than the cost of his crew. In fact, it would have been considered high even if I was just a regular client, not his friend working on trade.

I called Sal but suddenly, he was all business.

"Those were the costs," he told me.

There was no way I was going to continue to pay that rate, but now, I had a half-framed house and had just lost my mentor.

After paying Sal's guys, I had nothing left. There was no way I could hire another framer. So instead, I did what I had always done. I headed to the library and started teaching myself how to frame a house. I basically built the entire home on my own.

The funny thing about what happened with Sal was that the biggest lesson he taught me was the one where he screwed me over.

I remember that when it happened I called up my dad. I knew he didn't have a lot of money, but I figured he would at least call Sal a few names in Italian.

"Did you have a contract?" he asked.

"Well, no," I told him. "I shook his hand."

"You shook his hand?" my dad replied. "What is wrong with you? You can't shake a man's hand anymore, Joey. You need him to sign papers."

"But pop—" I started.

"Look, you got yourself into this, you get yourself out," my dad replied.

I was angry at the time, but he was right. Sal showed me that when it comes to money, you can't trust anyone. And as I soon learned, that included your own brother-in-law.

My family had known Joe Giudice's family since we were kids. It all started when we were in our 20s and Teresa started dating this guy Chris, who we all really liked. We figured they would get married someday - but then Teresa found out the guy was cheating on her, and that was that. Next thing we know, she starts dating Joe.

We were all kind of shocked. He was a rough guy, but he was also kind of like family. My parents and his parents had known each other a long time.

At first, we all got along. I liked Joe enough and Teresa and I had been best friends our entire lives. After she and Joe got married, we would all go out to dinner with my fiancée at the time. Our disagreements didn't begin until later.

But then I got into construction. Even though Joe had already become pretty successful in the business, he was still starting to act like I was some sort of rival, which was crazy because I was just this 23-year-old kid with a landscaping business.

After Sal quit on the house, it hit me that I had a lot left to do and didn't really know how to do it all.

Since Joe was in the stucco business, I reached out to him to help me with the stucco. So he comes in with his crew, they start working on the house - and then they also disappear. I had just gone from having a half-framed house to a half-stuccoed house. I was screwed.

Joe disappeared for months and then subcontracted the work to this other guy who only made it worse. Finally, I got rid of him and hired a new contractor. By that time, I had pulled together enough money to finish it myself.

I called my dad again.

"Whose house is it?" he asked me.

"What do you mean?"

"Is it your house or Joe Giudice's?" he asked.

"It's mine," I replied, annoyed by his tone.

"Then take care of your own damn house and don't worry about him."

I knew that family was more important than stucco, and that ultimately, my sister and her husband would be family long after I sold the house that was now driving me nuts. So I didn't say anything to Joe. I looked the other way and focused on getting the job done.

It took me two years to complete. I got cash advances and bartered for work when I could. I did what I had to do. I worked nights. I worked until two in the morning.

At the end of it all, I completed the house and moved in. I was a 24-year-old kid working in the landscaping business, and I had just built a two-million-dollar home on my own.

It wasn't Sal's house. It certainly wasn't Joe Giudice's. It was mine.

Just like in high school, I could let the trouble bring me down or I could get out of it. I could have sued Sal or gotten in a fight with Joe. I could have asked my dad to help or started talking shit about any of the guys who screwed me. But I didn't.

I got to work, and I got myself out of trouble.

Things are always going to go wrong. People are going to ditch out mid-job, and sometimes even when you have them sign papers they'll still screw you.

You can complain about it.

Or you can get to work.

As my father told me that day, "Chiodo scaccia chiodo!"

Basically: you'll get over it.

And I did. As soon as I moved into my own home, I forgot about what happened getting there. I was living in a palace that I'd practically built with my own hands, and I had become a better developer in the process.

That's the thing about trouble. We can learn from it.

So instead of being angry or being an ass, I took those lessons from Sal and Joe, and made sure to use them the next time I was building a property.

We get to decide how long we want to hold onto trouble. We can hang around and wait to get busted, we can blame everyone else around us, or we can just take care of it.

When we were growing up, there was no such thing as "cover your ass" because you just took care of it. You didn't whine and squirm and you weren't a rat. Everyone took care of their own.

You took the punishment, learned the lesson, and did it better next time.

I learned the lesson and I did it better next time.

I got contracts. I didn't bring in family members to help me. I continued to barter and trade, but I made sure I knew what I was getting for my work. I didn't want to be surprised by an invoice again. I made sure to agree to the price of service before I was stuck with a half-finished building.

And I did it all living in my two-million-dollar home. My first house - but certainly not my last. My business was growing and it was about to get a lot bigger, but first I had to figure what I was doing with my fiancée.

Once again, I had gotten myself into trouble and I had to figure my way out.

Gino and Joey hanging tough

Fam life on the boat

My little ballers

Date night with Melissa

The Gorga gang

My Antonia

Little beauty

A great night out

Hanging with the boys

Family vacation

Celebrating the holidays

City life

Football days

JOHN F. KENNEDY HIGH SCHOOL FOOTBALL ROSTER — 1991

Gorga #52

They grow up fast

Antonia and Gino before the game

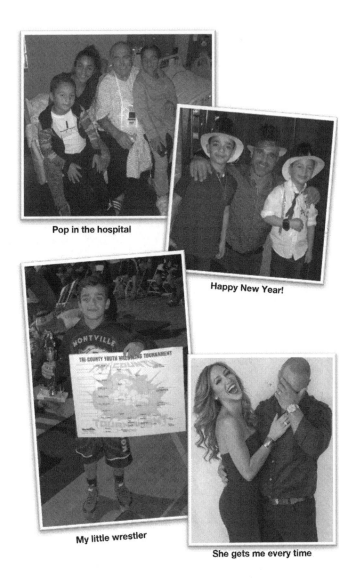

Pop in the hospital

Happy New Year!

My little wrestler

She gets me every time

Love of my life

Super model

Teresa and Gia

I love these kids!

Handsome dude

Hitting the runway

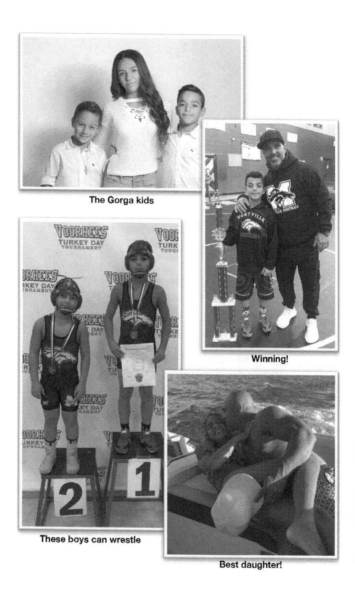

The Gorga kids

Winning!

These boys can wrestle

Best daughter!

Family forever

Life's a beach

Hottest girl in the club

Go Yankees

Jet set

Always loved her in a bathing suit!

Day in the life

Mom

Great night out

Melissa and Antonia back in the day

They're the best!

Don't drop that towel!

Doing the rounds

Married life

Grow with Gorga!

Hitting the gym

Not bad for 21!

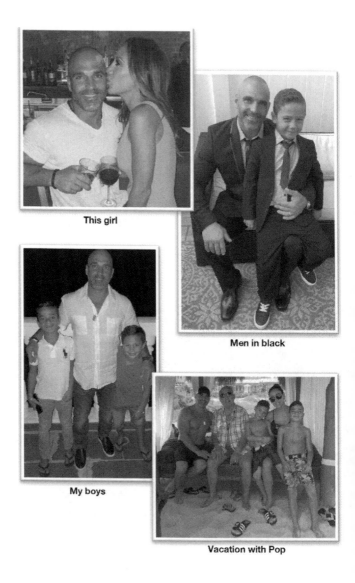

This girl

Men in black

My boys

Vacation with Pop

Just hanging

Selfie for two

The OG's – Original Gorgas!

CHAPTER 7

If You Have a Doubt, Get Out

So in my neighborhood, you met a girl, you went steady with her, and if your family liked her and you liked her, you got married, had a family, and stayed together till death do you part.

Which is why when I was 24, I decided it was time to propose to my high school sweetheart, Stacey. She was a great girl and I knew I loved her. The only problem was I didn't know if I was in love with her. I mean, what did I know? I was only 24. Plus, I really hadn't experienced much of life. All I did was work.

So we got engaged, and everyone was real happy for us. Except me.

I felt bad. We had been together eight years. We were best friends. I thought about calling it off but then her dad got sent to prison. I'm sure you can figure out why - we were Italians in New Jersey. So the wedding got postponed and I felt bad about ending it with her, pops being in jail and all.

But the second thoughts wouldn't end. I just wasn't sure what to do.

I was still running the landscaping business so I started talking to my customers about marriage, asking them how they felt about their wives.

One of my customers was this older guy, Gerry. He was in his 70s and super successful. So successful that he'd been married three times.

I figured Gerry would know a thing or two about getting hitched.

So one day we were sitting in the back of his house, looking at his pond.

I told him about my fiancée and our engagement. And then I told him about my second thoughts.

He looked at me real hard and said, "Let me tell you something, son. If you have a doubt, get out. The woman you're supposed to marry and spend your life with, you shouldn't have any doubts."

I nodded, knowing he was right. But I couldn't imagine breaking Stacey's heart like that.

Later that night, I went over to her house and her mother and sisters were all there. It was a few weeks before the wedding. They had brought home her wedding dress that day and they were all freaking out that I was going to see it. Her sisters were sitting around the kitchen table making wedding favors, and I could feel my heart in my friggin' throat.

How was I supposed to do this to such a nice girl? It didn't make sense.

The girls are all yelling at me to get out of the kitchen because the dress is in there. I go into the other room and I just can't end it. I pretend like everything is fine even though I am freaking out the closer we get to the wedding.

A few weeks later, I'm at my parents' house, helping my mom with something. Stacey calls me and tells me that we were supposed to do something that afternoon. I had totally forgot but the next thing I know, Stacey shows up at my parents' house, storms in - she doesn't even say hi to my parents - and starts yelling at me.

She storms back out of the house and I follow her but she gets in her car and leaves. I'm standing in my parents' garage and I'm thinking: "If that's what she's doing now, what will it be like once we're married?"

A few days later, I sat her down at my house. It was a month before the wedding. To this day, it is still probably one of the hardest things I have ever done.

I told her, "Look, Stacey, I love you and you're one of my best friends, but if we get married, I just don't think I'm gonna be happy. I want the woman I'm gonna be with, I want to hold her on a pedestal. You deserve that too, and I don't think I can give you what you deserve."

We were both sad. We cried and hugged. She went home and I thought she'd be okay. But within days, I hear she's going out with other guys. Friends are calling and asking if they can take her out.

About three months later, I'm barely going out. Instead, I'm starting to go crazy. I didn't just lose my fiancée; I lost my best friend.

I don't think anyone on the planet makes a tough decision like that and doesn't regret it. So three months later, I called up Stacey and told her I wanted to get back together.

"Joey," she told me, crying. "You broke my heart. My ma said it was like you died in our home. We loved you so much. It was like we had a funeral for you in our home."

It hit me again what I had done, but I knew it was time to move on.

And then the next year, I did practically the same thing with another girl.

I'm not kidding. And I'm not proud of it.

Six months after Stacey and I broke up, I met this other girl, Lisa. We had actually known each other for a long time, but we hadn't seen each other in years. Lisa's father was my sister's godfather, but we didn't live in the same town.

My heart was still broken, so in a way, I was just going through the motions.

The problem was that Lisa's father was so strict. We weren't even allowed to go out to dinner alone. We could only eat with her family.

Here I was working almost 90 hours a week and in order to even see my girlfriend, I had to have dinner with her whole family.

It was nuts but I liked the girl. It was only a couple of months in when her father pulled me aside and told me that if I was going to keep coming to his house, I needed to marry his daughter. Now, obviously I should have said no right there, but I was 25 and wasn't much smarter than I was at 24. I felt bad for Lisa. She was so beautiful but so sheltered, and I guess I thought I was saving her.

Six months later, I was down on one knee proposing. The funny thing was with both Stacey and Lisa, I didn't even pick out the ring.

My dad knew this jeweler, so I would ask him to go get me a ring and he would pick the ring out for me.

When I told him I wanted to propose to Lisa, he stopped me. "Are you sure you know what you're doing?" he asked.

"Of course," I told him. "Lisa's a great girl."

"I know she's a great girl," my father replied. "But you sure you're ready to get married to her?"

Something in me said no, but I remembered how heartbroken I was after Stacey, and I didn't want to make the same mistake again.

So Lisa and I got engaged - and then, just like that, it was time for the bridal shower.

Part of the tradition was that me, her father, and my father were all supposed to bring her to the restaurant for the shower.

I walk in with her and all the women are there. Her mother and sisters, all her friends. And I look around and I know I don't want to do this. I don't want to marry this woman.

I'm like, "Jesus, Joey. You can't do this again."

I leave the shower with my dad and Lisa's dad and we're all in the car, and I look at my father and I say, "Pop, I'm not getting married."

My father gets this sad look on my face, but Lisa's dad starts cracking up. He slaps the back of my head, laughing, thinking I'm kidding. But my father knows I'm being serious.

After the lunch, I bring all the gifts back to her house from the shower. She and I are outside and it's like déjà vu. I tell her that I can't do it, that I can't live my life feeling like this. I have too many doubts, and I know I won't be happy.

I broke another girl's heart.

The thing was, I knew a lot of people who had gone through with marriage knowing it wasn't the right choice for them and they were miserable. They woke up every day wishing they could change their lives but they had houses and kids and felt responsible for a decision they had made when they were 20.

A lot of them ended up getting divorced, and I didn't want to get a divorce.

I thought about what Gerry said: if you have a doubt, get out. And though I now have a daughter and can't imagine anyone doing that to her, I also knew that as difficult as decision as it was, it had been the right one.

The thing is, "if you have a doubt, get out" isn't just for broken engagements.

No matter how deep you might be into a deal, if something in your gut tells you it isn't right, you gotta listen.

And it's something I've had to use a million times more in business.

I'll be six months or even a year into a project and if something doesn't feel right, sometimes I just gotta walk away. Even if it's hard.

A year or so ago, Melissa, Teresa and I decided to open our own restaurant. My parents were such amazing cooks when I was growing up and Teresa and I wanted to use their recipes so we could always eat their food.

Before my mother got sick we had a place set up, but when she went into the hospital, we put everything on hold. We never signed the lease on the place. My mom was in the hospital for three months and we almost forgot about it.

But after she died, a friend of mine told me that he had a restaurant that was suffering and thought we might be able to partner up.

We thought it would be a good way to keep my father busy. He could go to the restaurant and work with the cooks. By this time, Teresa and I were cool again, and we had fun doing the restaurant together. Like I said before, we had always wanted to own a restaurant. So we went into business with my friends, and opened Gorga's.

The only thing was we didn't know how to run a restaurant. And we were both too busy to learn.

My father was going there every few days to work with the chef, but then he got sick and didn't go back.

Now none of us had the time for it, but our names were all over it.

I learned that if you don't have time to invest in a business you don't know anything about, then you shouldn't invest in that business.

I had way too many doubts and I knew we needed to get out. The place was so popular and the restaurant was really too small, so we agreed it made more sense to do it later when we had more time and found a bigger location.

So I went there one day and kind of like with Lisa and Stacey, I shut the business down.

It wasn't easy, but it's always better to walk away and burn one bridge rather than to stay and blow the whole thing up.

And I gotta say, whenever I think I can't walk away, that I've invested too much time or money or sweat, I just think back to Lisa and Stacey. Breaking up with them was real hard and I hated myself for it. But in the end, when I met the right one, I knew she should be my wife.

I didn't have any doubts and I have never wanted to get out.

Both Lisa and Stacey ended up finding guys that would put them on pedestals, and I know that, in the end, we were all happier for the hard decisions I made years before.

Whenever I worry about leaving a bad deal, I know that sometimes that's the only way to get to the right one.

CHAPTER 8

The Squeaky Wheel Gets the Grease

There is probably no truer saying in real estate. And in life.

Because the squeaky wheel does get the grease, and the guy who is willing to make the most noise is also the one who's probably gonna get what he wants.

Look, if you want, you can sit in the back of the room or the bar or whatever and play the cool guy, but the cool guy usually ends up broke and alone.

I never wanted to end up either, so when I see something I want, I don't sit back and wait for it to come to me. I go out and get it.

In the early 2000s after I broke up with Lisa, I started going crazy buying houses. I would buy them, rehab them and flip them - two, three, four-family houses.

Like my old mentor Sal, I was working on over 30 houses in just a couple of years. This was when people were getting mortgages left and right and I was turning properties everywhere. From the rough parts of Paterson to the fancy parts of Franklin Lakes, I was building across New Jersey.

And I wasn't doing it by being quiet.

I had learned that if you wanted to get anything done, you had to stand out. You had to be willing to make the call. And then call again. And again.

You had to be willing to show up in person.

You had to be willing to knock on doors until the right person answered.

And then you had to be willing to wine and dine that person until you got what you needed. But as I was about to learn, I could use those same rules in romance too.

Because I was about to meet the woman I would want to put on a pedestal forever.

Back to that big trip to Mexico where I met the future Melissa Gorga.

I had been doing nothing but working my butt off for months when some of my friends decided they wanted to go to Mexico for Spring Break. Because I was always working, I had never actually been on a Spring Break before. So there my friends and I go, all these 20-something guys partying with the college girls.

I'm 27 years old and I'm like a kid in a candy store. I'm having a blast, hooking up, and finally getting the chance to be a kid. It was one of the best times of my life. I'm in the pool with my best friend, Tony. We're hanging out with a couple of girls, but then I turn my head and I see this other girl. She's got big, curly hair and she's wearing that leopard bikini.

I watch her walk across the pool, and I tell my friend Tony: "That girl there, she's gonna be my wife."

I watched her go to hang out with her friends, but I was still hanging out with these other girls, and I didn't want to be rude. By the time they left, the girl in the leopard bikini was gone.

I walked over to her friends and asked about the girl in the leopard bikini. They all started teasing me, telling me I don't want her, I want them. We're all flirting and hanging out but the girl never comes back down to the pool.

I find out that they're also from New Jersey and we traded numbers. I could have left it at that. I could have forgotten about that girl in the bikini and never bothered to call her friends. But I didn't.

That summer, I was headed to the Shore and called to make plans with them. That's when they told me their friend's name was Melissa, so I asked if she would be there too. Her friend laughed. "You still thinking about her?"

At this point I didn't really go to clubs, but Melissa and her friends were younger, so I met up with them up at the clubs by the Shore. There were much younger kids there, guys and girls in their early 20s. I would get there early and leave early and sometimes I would see Melissa, but usually by the time she got there, I would be talking to another girl.

Other times, I just didn't have the balls to go up to her. Tony would tease me, and say: "We came all the way out here, go freaking talk to her."

But something in me said not yet.

That went on all summer. Every weekend I went, and I would wait, and she would come at different times. You would never see her talk to other guys. She was unapproachable.

Finally, summer came to an end, but I had been the cool guy in the back of the club, which meant I ended up alone.

I went back to work that fall with a vengeance. I mean, I was selling houses for $200,000 more than the asking price. I was building an empire. It was amazing. The real estate market was through the roof and I started partnering up with different guys, turning projects left and right.

But it also meant all I was doing was working. Flipping houses is a 24/7 job. You're trying to get that house on the market as soon as possible because every month you're not selling it, you're paying for it. It was such a crazy hustle trying to turn all those houses at once, so I started looking for real estate that would work at a slower pace. I knew it was time I get into bigger inventory, where I could sit back and collect rent, and not always be rushing towards a "For Sale" sign.

That's when I found the old mill building in Paterson. Good old Paterson.

Here's the deal about the squeaky wheel. I had started telling people I was looking for a big building. I didn't just keep that idea inside. I told my customers in the landscaping business. I told the agents I had been working with. And I told the attorneys.

And finally, I got that call. One of my customers, Frank, called me up and asked for a quote on a building he was working on in Oakland, NJ. He told me he had another property he was selling in Paterson but wasn't looking to get rid of it for another year because the building in Oakland wouldn't be ready until then. It was this old mill building. The first time I went and saw it, I knew we could turn it into apartment buildings.

The property cost $2.6 million, and the deposit was a fair percentage of that. The problem was that when you have 30 houses under construction, most of your money is in those houses, not in the bank, so I needed to come up with the cash or figure out another way to secure the building.

I suggested to Frank that I do the foundation for his new property in exchange for the deposit. Frank introduced me to one of his designers and over the next few months, we went to work. The architect showed me how to draw up plans on such a big project. We would get together, have drinks, and work.

Finally, the architect and the attorney and me, we present the plans to the town and we get approved for the 62 apartments. That's what brought me that night to Joey's. And that's when I walked in and saw my future wife, working as a bartender on a Thursday night.

No more Mr. Cool Guy from me.

I walked right up to her and told her she was gonna be my wife. But Melissa wasn't so sure. You break two engagements, word is definitely going to get around about you.

"Aren't you that guy who's been engaged 10 times?" she teased me.

But I was done sitting in the back, playing it cool, so I started telling her how I was going to put her on a pedestal. How I was going to make her my queen.

When that still didn't work, I started flirting with other girls, buying them champagne, making sure that Melissa was paying attention.

Still, by the end of the night, Melissa still wouldn't give me her number.

So I went back the next Thursday. Same thing. I told her I was going to marry her, and then flirted with other girls when she wouldn't believe me. Silly, I know. But we were just kids. And besides that, it worked.

I didn't go to Joey's the next week but my friend Tony did. When Melissa saw him, she asked where I was.

"Why?" Tony asked. "He told me you weren't interested."

"I didn't say I wasn't interested."

After Tony told me that Melissa asked about me, I went back the next Thursday.

I told her, "I'm not going to talk to you unless you give me your number."

She finally did, writing it down on a napkin, and for the rest of the night, I hung out at the bar and didn't talk to any other girls. When her shift was over, I invited her over, but she said no. Instead, I walked her to her car and called her later to make sure she got home safe. We ended up talking on the phone all night.

The next night, I invited her over for dinner, and she said yes.

So now for the wining and dining part. I wanted to make her this really special dinner. I mean, I had been asking this girl out for almost a year now, and here she was finally saying yes. But of course I ended up working late that night, so what could I do?

I ordered food from the best Italian restaurant in the neighborhood. I bring it to my kitchen and I make a real mess in there – pots and pans were everywhere. I even threw a little spaghetti sauce on the wall.

When Melissa came in, she was impressed.

"You've really been cooking in here?"

I smiled. "I wanted to make it special."

Because here's the deal. Whether you're wining and dining the new client or a new girlfriend, your job is to make yourself stand out.

Being the squeaky wheel isn't just about making noise. It's about making an impression.

And I wanted to make an impression.

My place was perfect – I had the candles lit, the fire going, wine and champagne out. I even set the table real nice.

It was like the best restaurant you could go to, and I knew Melissa was impressed.

My first house looked like a castle on the inside. There were these huge stucco walls, and I had murals painted on them of naked women. But not gross paintings. It was more like you were in an Italian museum than the Playboy Mansion.

Melissa loved the food, and I told her I had never made dinner for anyone else before, which was true (even if I didn't actually make the dinner).

Melissa still remembers me telling her that I wanted a mural of her too. I said, "You are just so beautiful, I am going to have my artist paint you on the walls."

She started laughing. "You're gonna put a picture of me up there?"

And I was like: "Yeah, why not?"

That's how much I wanted her.

All my friends were married, having families. But me, I was working all the time. And I had just broken up with Stacey and then Lisa. Between me and you, it had been a hard time. I'd go to my clients' houses, these big, beautiful mansions where these guys would be outside with the wife and kids. I wanted that too.

I would say: "One day, that's going to be me." I think that's why I kept getting engaged.

I just wanted it with the right woman. And I knew Melissa was the right woman.

She was 23 at the time. She'd just graduated college and was this young girl working three jobs, substitute teaching at the school and working a couple bartending gigs. She busts my balls now about telling her I was going to have her painted, but she fell in love with it.

When we were done eating, we went to my living room to watch TV. Normally I would've want to try something on her, but instead we just sat by the fireplace and talked. I put my arm around her and gave her a small kiss, but that was it.

I'll never forget that night. It just felt so good, like God had put us together.

And that was just the beginning. From that night, we started talking every day. We didn't leave each other's sides.

Melissa was a hustler like me. Her father passed away when she was 16 and she had to put herself through college. This girl, she was so impressive.

We lived an hour apart from each other and still saw each other every night. I would be so tired from working on all these houses and trying to get the apartment building going, and I would still drive an hour to see her. We would finally get to dinner and I would be passing out at the table, but I think we both knew what I was working for. We were gonna have a family together, and I wanted to make that family proud.

After a few weeks, Melissa quit her bartending job. We waited a few months to have sex but from the first night we did, we knew we were a fit. It was the most amazing feeling. Like we had been having sex together for 100 years.

The next day, I sent her 10 dozen roses. She'd never had any romantic thing like that. She walked up to her apartment and there were all these roses sitting there on the steps. She moved in a couple weeks later.

Tony and I went to her apartment and moved her out, and as soon as she got to my house, it felt perfect.

What I realized is that you gotta show people you care. You gotta go out of your way to make sure they feel special. And I wanted Melissa to feel special.

One night, I brought Melissa over to my house. My parents were worried because, as you know, I had done this before. She wasn't Italian in the way we were - we were truly Italians, new to America and still old-fashioned. Melissa was an Italian-American living in New Jersey. Still, Melissa loved family and was so respectful of my Mom and Pop that she fit right in.

Teresa and Melissa started off great too. My sister was super sweet and the two of them got along great. I also fell in love with Melissa's mother and sisters. Our families began to know each other, too.

I was getting so busy at work that I needed an office manager, and I knew Melissa was so smart that she'd be great for it. She was teaching in these rough neighborhoods at the time, so I asked her if she would work for me. That way, I told her, whenever we wanted to go on vacation she wouldn't need to ask her boss - because I was the boss.

She agreed, and that's how pretty much everything worked for us. The pieces just fit.

I wasn't the type of guy that spoiled girls, but I treated Melissa like a queen.

Because that's what being a squeaky wheel does. If you want something and everything is working to make it happen, then you better go out there and make it happen.

I've had real estate deals that just couldn't go right. But if there is a deal I really want to see happen, and everything is tracking great, I make sure I'm bringing my best to the table. You gotta be extra nice and friendly. You gotta work twice as hard. You gotta be sure you make it happen.

Which is why six months after dating, I go to my father and I ask him for another ring.

He tells me: "You go get the ring. You want her, you do the work."

He was right. If you want someone, or something, it's up to you to do the work.

So I went and picked out this big diamond for Melissa. I didn't even hesitate. I knew it was the right decision.

So I tell Melissa we're spending the weekend away and I get us a suite at this really fancy hotel with a beautiful spa and restaurant. Melissa goes to the spa while I put rose petals all over our room.

After her spa day, she comes back to the room and it's just covered in roses. I'm sitting there in a chair, and I get up and walk towards her and get down on one knee.

She's crying, I'm crying, and she says yes.

We make love right there on the rose petals. We have this crazy, passionate sex like we're never gonna see each other again, even though we're now getting married.

Right away, we start planning the wedding.

My mom was like: "What are you rushing for?"

But we both knew it was right. We didn't want to wait.

The squeaky wheel doesn't wait. And what some people call impatient, I call getting it done.

Melissa and I, we wanted to get it done.

Everyone was like: "Holy shit, he says he's getting married again."

But this time, I didn't have any doubts.

Normally the girl's parents pay for the wedding, but Melissa didn't have a father, so I paid for everything. Whatever she wanted. Her mother gave her a beautiful wedding dress.

I would have given her anything. I had my own home, I had real estate, but I never asked her for a prenup. Because when you love someone, and she's gonna be your queen, you forget the money. If I didn't trust her, I shouldn't be marrying her.

The day of our wedding, we go to a church in Franklin Lakes. We're there on the altar saying our vows and it's this beautiful sunny day. Then the priest turns to me, and says: "Repeat after me."

As soon as I start talking, it starts raining and storming outside.

After the ceremony, the priest says to me in Italian: "That was God saying, 'Thank God, he got married.'"

It was my 30th birthday, and it was the happiest day of my life.

But we wouldn't have gotten there had I stayed watching Melissa from the back of the club.

Just like the apartment building in Paterson, I had to fight for what I wanted, and I had to show I deserved it.

I deserved a girl like Melissa, and she deserved a guy like me.

Whether it's in business or relationships or partnerships or whatever else: when something fits, you gotta fight for it. You gotta be the squeaky wheel even if it drives people a little nuts. Because they'll be willing to get it done for you in order to get you off their backs.

Now, I'm not saying that's why Melissa said yes. But if I didn't treat her like a queen, would she have ever become mine?

I'm sure you know she wouldn't. She knew what she wanted, and together, we've been able to build that life together...even when life got tough.

CHAPTER 9

You Gotta Gamble

So back to that apartment building in Paterson. In real estate, you can't be scared. If you're afraid to pull the trigger, you're never going to make it.

Say you have $250,000 in the bank, but you need to spend $200,000 right now. If you're too afraid to use the cash and you're worried about your bank account balance, then real estate isn't for you. Like I say, the money in the bank makes no money. You can't live off one percent.

You gotta be willing to put your cash on the table even if that means you're taking a gamble. Real estate is like a big casino except in this one, the dealer is on your side. Because the banks and the big investors, they want you to win. If you win, they win. It's a safer bet, but it's still a bet.

After Melissa and I got married, she kept working for me in the office.

The big old mill building was still sitting there and I was waiting for my client to actually sell it to me. I'm still flipping all these houses, making money, investing it back out on the street. In the meantime, I sold my first house in Franklin Lakes.

I wanted to build Melissa our family home, but while we looked for the perfect property, we moved around between a few of my rentals.

We decided we wanted to move closer to our families, so we started looking at areas near my sister. I called a few people I knew and they told me about a perfect lot in Montville. Melissa and I went and took a look at it, and she was like: "This is it."

I bought the lot and had my architect draw up plans for our dream home, but I didn't tell Melissa. Instead, at Christmas I gave her a poster roll with a big bow on it.

"What is this, Joe?" she laughed. "A poster?"

But then she opened it up and pulled out the blueprints and the deed to the address.

She lost it. She was so excited.

It was 2006 when we started building the house. It's big and gorgeous and it's the same house we live in today. I work on it full-time when I'm not working on my other houses or trying to get my apartment building going.

Because I didn't have a lot of cash when I got into the apartments, we made a deal in the agreement that if I couldn't come up with the down payment, it could be tied to my home. At the time, that home was the one in Franklin Lakes, but now, that home would be the one we were building in Montville.

Whatever money I made went right back onto the street – into the houses I was working to flip, into the house I was building with Melissa, and into the old mill building that was beginning to get moving.

2006 turned into 2007 and there started to be some rumblings about the housing market. Things had been selling left and right but suddenly people were finding it harder to get a mortgage. I was having trouble moving some of the houses and then it was time for me to close on the building in Paterson.

Like I said, if I didn't close on the building, they took my house. The stakes were high.

Melissa and I already have one child at this point with a second on the way. And the economy is slowing down. I'm under construction on, like, 30 homes and I'm trying to get the house done in Montville so Melissa and I can move our growing family into the new home.

I had to close the deal by September 12.

Because I had negotiated myself into that apartment building using my house, I needed to negotiate my way through the deal without losing it.

Meanwhile, everything is starting to change. Melissa and I finish the house in Montville. We don't finish every room, but it's good enough. We don't have a lot of money and this is a big house, so there are all these empty rooms with just a little bit of furniture.

I start working with a bank on the Paterson deal. They commit to the project and we start doing all the paperwork - the appraisal, the environmental.

Then, two months before I have to close, CNN airs a report that the real estate bubble has burst. I don't know what's about to happen, but it starts happening fast.

Overnight, I can't even get people to come and see houses that before had been selling in days. The bank that was going to do the loan on the apartment building backed out, keeping my deposit money.

Even if you are under construction, the banks are pulling out.

The only thing I had on my side was that I had been able to get a Temporary Certificate of Occupancy, or a TCO.

But the banks still wouldn't help me. They wanted $300,000 up front, which I didn't have.

Finally, I found this guy in Manhattan. His name was Murray and he lived on the top floor of this major high-rise he owned. I tell him my deal, what's going on with the apartments, and about the hard cash loan.

He tells me to pick him up the next day to go see the property.

The next morning, I pick him up at 9:00 am and we drive out to Paterson. As soon as he gets in my car, the guy falls asleep. So we drive out to the mill building in silence until we arrive.

"Murray," I nudge him. "Murray."

He wakes up and sort of figures out where he is. I start to get out of the car but Murray just rolls down the window and looks out at the building.

He turns back to me and says: "Let's go."

"Are you sure you don't want to look inside?" I ask. I'm freaking out because I'm guessing from just one look, Murray doesn't like the building.

"No, I'm okay," he tells me. "We can head back now."

As soon as I pull out of the lot, Murray has fallen back to sleep. I start thinking how I'm going to break the news to Melissa. I'm convinced that they're going to end up taking our house...the one we just built and moved into.

I'm going nuts. I'm strapped to a wall and there is nothing I can do. And in the meantime, old Murray is taking a nap in my passenger seat.

Finally, we're making our way back through Manhattan when Murray wakes up. He turns to me as I'm driving and says: "I'll do it."

I don't even know what to say. Here I am thinking that everything is lost. But no matter what, I knew I couldn't give up now. I would do whatever it took to close that loan and to keep my house. The next day, Murray's attorney called me and told me that the loan would be for $2.55 million, with five points at 15%.

It was a rough deal, but it was what I needed to get into the building and save my home.

Sometimes the negotiation is in your favor; sometimes, you negotiate just to survive.

The day I closed the building, Melissa went into labor and my son was born. I put an Eli Peyton NY Giants jersey on him and an hour later, I go to my attorney's office to close on that building. I had $3,000 left in my bank account. Nothing was selling, I had houses everywhere, and I had no cash to invest in the 62-unit building I had just bought at a 15% interest rate.

But I wasn't afraid. I knew that if I could ride out the storm, I'd end up on the other side. The next day, I used the $3,000 to hire a contractor to do the demo in the building. I could have let the other houses on the market go. They could have gone into foreclosure or short sale but I didn't want to do that to my investors. I wanted to hold up my end of the deal.

I went to the banks and told them I was going to finish up the homes. I wasn't going to foreclose on them, but I need them to back me up. I hired auction companies to come and do auctions on the houses like they were in foreclosure, all so I could sell them off without giving them back to the bank. One by one, I began to pay the banks back.

I was able to get rid of the inventory and I rented out the two I couldn't sell. Meanwhile, I'm doing this while I'm trying to build this other building.

Melissa and I, we went from living a good life with all the perks and the credit cards to being on a crazy budget. We had two kids and I had to give Melissa an allowance of $100 a week for groceries and gas. I knew she hated it. I hated it too, but it was what we had to do.

There were times when Melissa would call me saying, "We have no diapers." One night, we go to Costco because the diapers are cheaper there. We get a big box and some milk and we go to ring up and they ask for my Costco card. I give it to them and they tell me the card is expired.

I'm like, "Okay, so what?"

They tell me that we need to renew our membership and that it's $100.

Problem is, I only have $70. Here I am building this 10-million-dollar building, we live in a million-dollar home, and we can't afford diapers.

We had to leave Costco and go to another store because I couldn't afford to renew a $100 membership.

Melissa was my ride or die the whole time. Sure, she was worried. She would ask me if we were going to get out of it and I would always tell her yes, but I wasn't sure.

I just kept rolling the dice, working to keep us at the table. I started working on the building and found out it had all these cast iron radiators. I cut them out and made $1,800 from them. I started pulling other stuff out of the building I could scrap. I'd make just enough money to keep the crew working for a few days.

I'd drive up in the morning and there would be contractors waiting outside, wanting to get paid. It was a bad time for all of us in construction. Everyone was hurting. We had all been making money before it all suddenly dried up.

Some guys didn't make it. They jumped from their high-rise buildings. But I looked at my wife and kids and knew we had to keep going. I started pulling metal out of the building so I could pay the contractors. I would drive around looking for scrap metal. If I saw a washing machine on the side of the road, I would grab it.

I would use anything I could find to pay the guys. I knew that once I got people in that building, we were going to be fine. I just had to get us there.

Then I realized that I could find more than scrap out there. We needed cabinets and kitchen hardware for the units, and one day, I'm driving past this property and it has foreclosure signs all over. There are cabinets in the dumpsters. All of these cabinets. I took the doors and the cabinets and the toilets back to the building. Just like I had once done with the kitchen equipment, I start refurbishing all of it so I could use it in the building. I painted the toilets and cleaned them inside and out. I sanded the cupboards, and painted them white. Piece by piece, we started putting the units together.

After six months of doing construction, a bank came in to help. Because I did right by all the banks and got rid of all the inventory, one of the banks was open to helping me with the hard loan guy. Six months later, they paid Murray out in full and loaned me another million for construction. Instead of paying 15% on the loan, I was paying 5%. I got the loan in draws so the more work we did on the building, the more we were able to pull out.

I started negotiating with the town. That building had been standing there empty for so long that they were motivated to get people in it. I asked them if I could rent the top floor and work my way down. It took me about two weeks of meeting with the mayor and the construction office and the regent, explaining what I had been through to save the building, for them to give in. I told them that if this building didn't get done, it would be an eyesore, and they agreed.

They said that if it had sprinklers on the top floor, and two ways to exit, I could rent it.

One night, I came home and Melissa started crying.

"What's happening to us?" she asked. "I can't even go to the store to buy food."

I told her, "I don't control what happens in the world, but you got to believe in me, I will get us out of this."

Finally, we started getting calls for the top floor and we started renting the units. They were large with these great big windows and they looked gorgeous.

We only had the freight elevator, which everyone would have to use. Since it was dangerous, I gave this guy free rent to run the elevator whenever anyone needed it.

One day, the elevator broke down. One of the tenants had just had knee surgery and so me and another guy would pick her up and carry her up and down the stairs.

Here I am trying to put out all these fires and complete the building and not go broke, and in the middle of it, I am carrying this lady up and down the stairs.

All the tenants saw how hard I was working, so they gave me a chance. They were people from the inner city, just like the people I'd grown up with, and the inner city has heart. I finished that building one floor at a time until I was completely done. It was the biggest gamble of my life but, in 2009, when no one was giving loans, the bank refinanced the building. With the loan, I was able to buy the building next door and built 55 units there.

I was building an empire, and empires don't happen overnight. And they definitely don't happen by playing it safe.

They weren't easy gambles but the odds were a lot better than Vegas. And once I was done with both buildings, I was making rent in my sleep.

Everything began to turn around. We weren't just able to buy diapers; we were able to start living nice again, nicer than we had ever lived before.

We went on vacations and bought our kids toys. Melissa could go shopping again without having to think about what was in the bank account.

Just as quickly as it all came to a horrible stop, the train started again. But what I learned in that process, what helped me to survive the whole time, was how I negotiated the deal, and how I negotiated with other people. Because in real estate and in life, you're always negotiating. Every day, you're saying: "I can give you this for that."

My job was to make it seem like people were getting more than they were giving. Even if that wasn't the case.

By the time we had the second building up and running, people started calling me about warehouses for sale. I was known for converting these old mill buildings, and instead of making income off two to three to even 30 units at a time, I started making income off of hundreds.

It wasn't an easy gamble. But as I'll show, if you manage it right, real estate will always pay off.

CHAPTER 10

Push Hard and Play Nice

People are like Play-Doh. They're tough but you can still push them around. The thing is if you push too much, splat. You won't get anywhere with them.

After that first building, I began to get my system down. It wasn't so different from when I was flipping houses. They just had more people, more steps, more Play-Doh.

The thing is, as long as I pushed hard but still played nice, most of the time I could turn the ugliest building into a masterpiece. And that's what I started doing.

I found another great building out in Hawthorne. Of course, I was the only one calling it great. All my friends were saying, "Joe, you're crazy. You're gonna have to knock that thing down."

There were parts I brought down but I recycled the brick to reface the entire building, I restored all the hardwoods, and I reused all the materials I could from the old building. In the end, that thing was beautiful.

Those same friends came to the ribbon-cutting with the mayor and they were all, "Joe, what did you do to this thing?"

I paid $1.2 million for it, and now it was worth $10 million.

But that kind of job isn't easy. It takes a lot of hard work and almost as many signatures.

I moved into multiple apartment deals. I never wanted to wait for the next deal. I got into the apartment business to create wealth, to give my children something.

I had to give up my childhood. I didn't get to live as a kid; I had to work. I didn't want my children to miss out like I did. I wanted them to learn how to work hard, but I wanted to give them a company where they would always have a job and where they could always make money.

After I finished the first two buildings, I started flipping apartments like I was flipping homes.

I'd look for old buildings in neighborhoods already zoned for residential. They were these great, big warehouses, but I'd make sure there were houses around them, so we weren't stuck out in some industrial area where no one wants to live, or where we were gonna have to fight to get permitting.

Then I'd connect with my architect and get a survey of the property. My architect would make the calls to the city, the inspectors, and the zoning department. Usually we'd get a thumbs up, but just like my old client said, if we had a doubt, we'd get out.

If the building looked like a cute girl in a leopard bikini, we'd move forward. We'd check out the size of the building and the parking. Then we'd call the city and see if they liked the project.

See, the whole thing about playing nice is you gotta let the other guy think it's his idea. You don't want to always come in with a hard sell because then people start questioning it - they wanna find the hole in your plan.

But if you ask them if they like the plan and see what they think about it first, then they'll probably say, "Sure, looks great."

It's always easier to get a yes when you ask a question. It's harder to get a yes when you're telling someone what to do.

It's like I said: if you're getting all green lights on something, then you better make sure you're doing it right. But if I start getting red lights, if the town gives me a lot of resistance, the zoning guy says it's no good, or the school districts are overwhelmed, I walk away.

You can't be afraid to walk away.

Like I said, real estate is a gamble, and sometimes, the roll just isn't going your way.

But when it is, or when you know the deal is going to be worth the fight (like that first big building in Paterson), then you gotta lock it down.

You hire the architect. You find a good attorney the town's board likes. You gotta get to know all the players, become friends with the attorneys and the planners and all the people who are either going to make your life really easy or really hard.

You wanna play nice with all of them and find out the people they like to play with.

You want to swim with the right fish.

You don't go in with an outside attorney. Again, it's a sign of respect to not be pushing your ideas on other people. Come in with the guy they like and they'll feel like you're hearing them out.

Once you get your architect and your engineers and your attorney working, you go to the board.

If you've been doing everything right, if the property is a solid deal, you should get approved. In 45 days, you get the resolution and you're ready to go.

Then the real work begins.

You go through the permit process, and so much of that is getting charged to do work. It takes a lot of time and it's expensive. Your job is to negotiate your way through the process, trying to keep costs low while still securing what you need from the permit office. After you get permits, you start calling in the construction guys and the inspectors. I try to meet all the inspectors before they go out to the site.

Again, push hard but play nice.

An inspector can cost you time and money if they don't like what they see, or, just as importantly, if they don't like you.

I talk to the inspectors, let them know the other projects I've done. I let them know I'm on their side.

Look, an inspector can make your life miserable. If the guy didn't get laid the night before, you know you're going to have problems. Sometimes the inspector can be irrational. Sometimes they'll drive up to the building and then take off and say you weren't there... when you were standing right in front of them. You have a lot of money on the line and now you have two weeks to get the guy back out to the site.

And you're dealing with six different inspectors. You might get five great ones, but that sixth inspector can be the problem.

I make peace with them. I try to be friendly with them. If the guy has a bad attitude, I butter him up. We become buddies.

And I get a lot more passed inspections because of it.

The thing is, as much as you hope that everything's gonna run smooth, sometimes it just doesn't.

You might dig for a sewer line and it's nowhere to be found. You'll need to shut down streets and go into people's backyards.

There is always something that can delay you.

Because anything can happen in real estate.

Contractors will say they'll be there with 20 guys and then not show up. They might jerk you around the whole week. And the worst part is you already gave him a deposit, so you're just stuck there waiting.

Then you have to deal with OSHA, the Occupational Safety and Health Administration. I'm all onboard with having a safe site, but OSHA doesn't come in and say: "You need this kind of strap and we'll be back out to make sure you got it."

No, they just come in with their little ticket books and fine you for everything they see.

Then you have to go back to the town with all your paperwork and push there while still playing nice to make sure everything is signed off on so you can get your Certificate of Occupancy.

Development is hard. It's one thing to go in and flip a house. It's a whole other thing to try to build a multi-unit complex.

But I've never been afraid of hard work.

I'm used to getting up at five in the morning and driving out to the site.

I've got my work boots on and my truck and my cup of coffee and we're out there building this beautiful thing.

Sometimes it might take a year to get a project done. They all take time, money, a lot of faith, and a lot of hard gambles.

It's gonna take pushing hard and playing nice.

But then you're done and you get to stand back and watch the people moving in. You start seeing the checks roll in. You're paying $10,000 a month on the mortgage but you're making $100,000 in rent. And once you're done, you're done. You've got other people taking care of the property. You're paying them out a fraction of your profit, you're pulling equity and you're building the next one.

You're pushing hard and you're playing nice.

And you're building an empire.

CHAPTER 11

Every Deal Has Its Struggle

In 2011, when the TV producers first called us about *The Real Housewives of New Jersey*, I was confused.

"What do they want with us?" I asked Melissa.

I found out it went back to Teresa. She had filmed the show for a year and not once mentioned her brother, Joey. The show had aired but it was only the first season. People were just getting into the series.

For the years leading up to the show, my family hadn't been getting along so well. It was sad really. Joe Giudice and I had tried to work together a few times and it never went well. Then I started making money, and I think Joe didn't like that.

He had been in the business longer and here I was, this young kid flipping million-dollar houses and 10-million-dollar buildings.

We all used to go to the Shore together and Teresa and Melissa had been close, but by the time the show came around, we really weren't hanging out that much.

I gotta tell you, there is nothing harder than for an Italian family to not be close.

The worst part is it made it hard on my parents. Teresa was their little girl. My ma was really close with Teresa's girls, so it felt like my parents picked her over me.

Melissa and I were just sort of left on our own with our own family.

I had always imagined us all being together – my folks, Teresa, Joe, their kids, Melissa and our kids.

So when Teresa landed the show and didn't even tell us, I was sort of like, "What's going on over there?"

I didn't really know much about it. I work so much and I'm not the kind of guy who watches reality TV. I watch the Giants, not the Kardashians.

I didn't even really know what it meant.

So I was even more confused when they called us.

I guess once they found out Teresa had a brother, they were wondering what the story was. I mean, what kind of Italian doesn't mention her brother?

They found Melissa and me on Facebook and reached out. I'm sure it didn't hurt when they saw that Melissa was gorgeous.

But like I said, when they said they wanted to meet with us, I figured it was just to have us on an episode or something.

It was Melissa who explained it to me. "No, they want us on the show. Like regulars."

I really had no clue what we were getting into. It took me a month to decide. I was so nervous I broke out in hives. I didn't know if I wanted to do it. I was mad at my sister. I felt like she abandoned me. How are you on this important thing and you don't even call your brother? But Melissa wanted to do it.

Over the first 10 years of our marriage, I had asked so much of Melissa. From living in six houses in one year to not being able to buy diapers to leaving the house every morning at five and coming home late at night.

And now, she was asking me to do this.

How could I say no?

Melissa and I talked with the producers, and the producers liked what they saw.

I didn't really know much about how this stuff worked.

I just thought it would be fun for Melissa to get dressed up and be on TV.

Some of the stuff that's come to us from being on the show is amazing. We get to travel and meet people all over the world who love the show. We get to go to the front of the club and we always get a table. And sure, we've made some money from it too.

We all signed the contracts and started taping. We still had no clue how it was about to change our lives.

The first week of taping happened to be my son's christening, so they decided to film it for the second episode.

In Italian families, the christening is like a wedding. You rent out a big hall and there are tons of people there – family, friends, people from the community.

Melissa and I are there and Teresa and Joe are there, and as those who have watched the episode know, it did not turn out well.

I lost my mind. My heart was just broken. It was cracked into a million pieces because my family was not getting along.

That night when Melissa and I got home we cried and cried. It was a really rough time.

The show was so real. None of that stuff was made up. But the tough thing was that Melissa was loving it. She was doing the photo shoots and appearances but she was also the one who got along with her family.

Then things started changing in my home too. Before the show, Melissa had been a stay-at-home mom. She cooked us dinner and took care of the kids. It's not that I didn't want her to work, it's just that everything changed so fast. And our marriage started to change too.

It was hard. I missed my old Melissa. Now she was becoming a star, people were telling her how great she was, and she was out there doing these promotional things.

And I still had a job to do, except my job was getting even harder.

People saw us on TV and thought we were these big millionaires, but really, we were just the same people we were before. I was out there trying to do deals and I had to make sure I was really doing things right, that I wasn't getting screwed.

People think I'm a movie star, but I'm really just an Italian kid from Paterson.

But again, the work is what saved me. Because no matter what was going on at home or on the show or with my family, I would get up in the morning and head to work.

I realized the show wasn't forever. It was just there for a little while.

And remember what I said: life is all about moments, and I wasn't going to change my life for one little one.

I would go to the red carpet and the next day I would go to work.

Because every deal has its struggle. You got to work through the tough parts to get to the good ones.

There's an old Italian saying: "Quando finisce la partita il re ed il pedone finiscono nella stessa scatola." It means: When you finish the game, the king and pawn end up in the same box.

You just gotta walk through the dark times because we're all going to end up in the same box. We can make the bad day or the hard deal into something worse than it is, or we can get up the next morning and figure out our way through it.

Since the show started, Melissa and I have gone through a lot of bad days. But we've also had the best times of our lives.

And work. Well, I never stopped working. I started doing 200-unit buildings and then turned back to some of the smaller projects. I kept mixing it up because as soon as you get bored, you lose your steam.

And I wasn't going to lose my steam, whether at work or in my marriage.

I had to keep this popping.

Because every deal has its struggle, but it's always worth it in the end.

CHAPTER 12

You Always Got
to Be a Magician

You ever seen that movie *50 Shades of Grey* where the guy tosses his girl around and makes her feel like she's the only woman in the world?

That's how I wanna love my wife every day.

Look, I'll be honest: marriage is hard.

We fell in love a long time ago and I want us to stay in love.

Love is like business: if you're not constantly showing up to make it happen, it's gonna fall apart.

You always gotta be a magician.

Before we started the show, we'd come home and make dinner. Melissa was this cute little wife. We were so hot for each other, we used to have sex every day. Not kidding, for the first 10 years we were together, we had sex every day. Even after the kids came.

A lot of people, they have kids and they have sex less and less. They turn the kids into an obstacle. They've got the kids in the bed and they don't find time for each other.

Then you wonder why people start looking around. I never want my wife to crave for anything. And I never want to crave for anything.

You have to be gentle with your wife, but you also have to fuck your wife.

Kind of like push hard and play nice, but in bed.

And then you gotta put your wife on a pedestal. I remember when Melissa and I first got married and we were living in Franklin Lakes. It was like an hour-and-a-half away from her family, and I felt so bad about it.

So one weekend, we go down to the Jersey Shore, and it's like 30 minutes from her family, and they all come out and we have this great time. The next weekend, we go down and I have an agent show us a few places and we buy this cute bungalow.

I was like a magician pulling a rabbit out of a hat.

Melissa was so excited. We had so much fun in that house over the years. Her family would come out, and this was when Teresa and I were still close, so we would have this great time.

At the time, I didn't really have the money to pull it off - but you can't let money stop you from doing the right things. That goes just as much for when you've got a lot of money as for when you've got nothing.

Melissa and I had such a good time in those first years. It was real, and it meant something. We just had each other.

After the show started, there were all these other people in our lives. They were these demons. They were whispering stuff in Melissa's ear, telling her she was gonna be the next Jennifer Lopez, and I had to fight to keep my wife.

It's sad because you start off being a really sweet person, but now you gotta have tough skin because people are always talking about you.

You got the devil on your shoulder telling you your wife could leave at any time, and you think, man, maybe I should just get out of here before she breaks my heart. But it's the same way in business. You can't just walk away from something you invested 10 years of your life in because you get scared.

You gotta hustle to make it work.

I'm lucky because Melissa is such a strong woman. Even though she sometimes gets sucked into the fame, she always comes back. She knows what's important and together, we remind ourselves about who we are.

The Italians say, "L'amore vince sempre." Love conquers all.

Melissa and I work really hard to keep that love alive. We take the time to still have crazy, passionate sex together. Just this Christmas, I surprised her with a new wedding ring because, no matter what, she's still my bride.

I treat her like my queen because she is my queen, and I show up like a magician, pulling bunnies from a hat.

Which is why every day I come home and leave my work at the front door. Tomorrow, I'll go out and do battle, but tonight, my home is my peace. I'm there to be with my wife and my kids, and I gotta leave work alone.

But love doesn't just conquer all at home.

I gotta bring that love to my job every day too.

Because there is always something going on. Something always costs something, and the money isn't always there. You're always jumping between deals trying to make it happen, and you gotta be a magician at work too.

The thing is, once we got on the show, my job got harder. I needed to be super careful about who I did business with and how I acted. I'm under a microscope and yeah, there are times it makes me mad. Like I said, I've never cried so much. I would sit in my car and cry. I had this shit with my family, and I was worried about Melissa, and I still had my business to take care of.

I didn't want to become a different person. I wanted to stay true to who I was. And to my work and to my wife.

I decided that nothing was going to change me. I came from nothing and I'm gonna go back to nothing, I thought. I am going to get up and do the same routine. I'm gonna stay Joe Gorga, that inner city Italian kid from Paterson. And I'm gonna stay focused on my work, even if it got a little tricky once I got on the show.

I'm not selling perfume, you know - it's not like that in real estate. People feel a little weird buying a house from someone they know from TV.

And everyone thinks they know you when you're on TV.

So I had to start really hustling, getting more stuff out there, changing it up. I started looking for new properties, making them work. I have everything from inner cities to high-end. The thing is, if you have a good project in an inner city, you're never empty. In the nicer areas, they take more time, and they can be more difficult.

So I just started working even harder.

That's why Teresa and I started the restaurant, because we always wanted to run our own thing. And that was the crazy thing about the show - it started to bring my family back together.

It was really hard for the first four years, but we had to work together and we had to talk about the issues. Instead of just being angry, we had to start working it out. And we started hanging out again – my sister and my parents and my nieces.

I had to be a magician there too. I had to start for-
giving and making things okay with Teresa because
she was my only sister.

Then Teresa went to prison.

It was a terrible time for all of us. She had walked a
straight line her whole life. She respected the law. She
was raised the right way. And all of a sudden, she's
going to jail?

I was driving in my car when I heard the news. It
was on the radio, and I found out from the radio. I
pulled over and just started crying.

It felt like our lives were being destroyed.

But I knew we couldn't give up.

I called Teresa to let her know I was there for her
and I would help her however I could.

There was still anger between us at the time, and
she was going through all this pressure with Joe and
the courts and now jail. And she was so cold with me.

I think she was afraid so she really didn't let me in.
That was hard. It made the whole thing even sadder.

My sister was going to jail and there was nothing I
could do about it.

I called her the day she was supposed to report. I
remember I was out working at a site because we had
tried to lay sod a few days before and it had frozen
over. So I'm there by myself on a Sunday morning,
trying to break up this frozen sod. I'm picking away at
it, and it's taking forever.

I get on the phone with Teresa to tell her I love her and to try to support her however I can, and she just starts yelling at me, telling me it's my fault she's got this sentence.

And I'm just shocked and heartbroken and pissed.

We hang up and I'm out there all day, working on this sod, and I'm crying and yelling swear words. I'm so angry and sad and now I have to go home and live with her words.

My mother would visit Teresa every week and would tell me Teresa was asking about me.

I didn't want to go, but I also knew it was time to pull the rabbit from the hat.

I had to show up for my sister, and I had to forgive.

As soon as I pulled up to the prison, I see the barbed wire and I'm trying to hold back the tears. I know I need to be strong for my sister, but once I see all the security and I get inside and see the other inmates, I just start bawling inside.

Then I see my sister through the doors, and I can't hold it in anymore.

Tears were everywhere. My sister was crying along with her daughter Gia and I.

Teresa and I hugged and we had a great conversation, and though I could tell the place had made her a little harder and a little colder than she was before, I felt like I was finally hanging out with my sister again.

Now, we're finally back together like when we were kids.

Her Joe is away in prison, and I've been able to show up for Teresa and her girls. I get to be a magician for the whole family. I get to surprise them and fix what used to be broken.

Over the years, I've gotten to fix my relationship with my dad too. We never brought up what happened that night of the christening. We just continued to do what we normally did. And now he takes rides with me to stay busy.

Later I told him, "You gotta remember, I'm your son. You ignored me and you took someone else's side."

I know he loves me, and he tells me he's proud of me.

Because I'm not the only one who knows how to surprise people.

At the end of the day, the money doesn't matter. The fame doesn't matter. None of it matters unless you have your wife and your kids and the people you love. That's what all the work is for, so without them, what are you doing it for?

Melissa and I, we've never given up on our marriage. We come from people who stay married, and we've been determined to make it work for us.

It hasn't been easy, but we're doing it.

I keep surprising her - in the bedroom, through gifts, through staying true to each other. I think that's what's kept both of us real.

CHAPTER 13

Put Your Head Down and Just Keep Running

I don't care how old you are. You can be eight or 38 or 58 and still want the love and support of your parents. You could be making a billion dollars a year but if your parents don't tell you they're proud of you, or if they don't show you that they love you, it will never feel like enough. After the christening, it was hard with my parents. Like I said, my dad and I didn't talk about it, and it didn't make the situation any easier.

My mom and I had our own thing. My mom had always been on Teresa's side, and I understood that. Teresa is her daughter and Italians always think that girls need the support and that the guys should be able to take care of themselves. And when grandkids come around, grandmas are always closer to their daughters' kids, because Italians think those are the kids that share your blood. As much as I love being Italian, we've got some screwed up stuff.

My dad and I put the christening behind us but my mom held a grudge. Still, over the years on the show, we got close again. I mean, she was my mom. She was like a little baby to me. I loved her so much.

The thing is, my mother was never sick.

When we were growing up, my pop had the health issues. We were always so worried about him. He had a heart attack when he was 39 and I remember when I was a kid, every time I saw an ambulance I would worry they were coming for my dad.

My mom was the healthy one.

But you know, people get older. My mom had rheumatoid arthritis and one day, she collapsed in the kitchen.

So we go to the hospital and they tell us that she has pneumonia. She gets admitted into the hospital but she's so uncomfortable in the bed because of the arthritis that we're all rubbing her legs and arms trying to make her feel better.

My father was pretty sick himself, but he was there every day because my mother was his queen.

We're thinking she'll pull through in a couple of days and be home, but then three days later, she's intubated. Everyone's upset, and we start staying with her around the clock. My dad would be there all day, and then my sister would come in that afternoon until late at night when I would take over for the graveyard shift, all until my dad showed up the next day.

No matter what had happened to us as a family, we were all there together.

It didn't matter how much I had worked that day or what was going on, I was going to be there for my mom.

I remember when I played football, my coach used to tell me to grab the ball, put my head down, and just keep running.

That's all I could think about as I drove to the hospital every night. They brought in another bed for me, but sleeping in a hospital is never easy.

My mom was unconscious with this tube down her throat, and every night, I would come and sleep next to her, just watching to make sure she was okay.

My mother had all kinds of rashes and sores from being in the bed, so I would move her around, trying to get her back to being herself.

She was like that for two months. And for two months, we kept that same routine. I didn't feel like I was alive. We were just going through the motions. Sleeping there all night, I was barely seeing my wife and kids.

The doctors were worried about her having a stroke so they took out the tube. We tried to wake her up but she wouldn't come to, so they had to put the tube back in.

It was crazy. Two months before, she was fine, and now we couldn't get her to wake up.

Then one day, she woke up. It was amazing, but she was really weak. She couldn't be left alone, so we all just gathered around her. She seemed to be getting better.

After thinking we were gonna lose her, we start to have hope. They move her to rehab and my sister and I started telling my pop she'd be coming home soon.

We kept our same shifts – my dad in the morning, my sister in the afternoon, and me at night. She was getting better and we were all excited.

Then one morning, my father shows up at 5:00 am as usual. Two hours later, the hospital calls me.

"Mr. Gorga," they tell me. "Your father is on his way to St. Joe's in Wayne, NJ. He got sick at the hospital and they called the ambulance."

Here's my dad visiting my mom at the rehab, and now he's in the hospital.

I rush to St. Joe's to see my pop.

He's all worried about my mom.

"Is she okay?" he keeps asking.

"Yeah, she's fine," I tell him. "Now we're worried about you."

Two hours later, the rehab calls me and tells me my mom is sick too.

"It's pneumonia again," they tell me. "We're going to be moving her to St. Joe's in Paterson."

So I got one parent at St. Joe's in Wayne and the other at St. Joe's in Paterson.

My dad had been at the hospital all week, washing my mom down, kissing on her, and he had no clue he was sick.

My sister and I decide not to tell my dad. We're hoping she'll just be back in the rehab by the time he gets better.

Teresa goes to be with mom, and I stay with dad.

Now I'm not working at all. My sister and I are switching between both parents, and Melissa is helping out in between.

My father has pneumonia, but he's going to be okay. He wants to talk to my mother, but we don't want him to know how sick she is. We keep thinking she's going to get better.

We tell him she's busy in therapy or out of the room. We did this for a week-and-a-half straight.

My mother had the tube in her for five days, but she started do better.

They decided to pull the tube and were getting ready to move her to a regular room.

I hadn't been to work in almost two weeks. I had never done that before unless we were on vacation, but what else was I going to do?

All we could do was put our heads down and just keep running.

Teresa and I, it was like we were kids again. It was just our little family trying to make it, and we were going back and forth between our parents.

But our dad was getting better and our mother was getting better, so we were thinking they'd be back together by the end of the week.

Then, two days later, Teresa calls me.

"Mommy wants you here," she tells me. "She wants you by her side."

I'm like, what's going on? But I rush over to St. Joe's and get to her room and they've moved her back to ICU.

I walk in, and Teresa is in tears. The doctors are telling us that we might only have a couple of hours with her. They ask us to sign "Do Not Resuscitate" papers, but we refuse to sign anything.

We want our mom to get better. She was getting better.

I go to her bedside, but she isn't responding.

I grab her hand, and I start crying, begging her to fight.

"Please Mommy," I cry. "I love you so much. Please."

But she didn't want to fight. She had been fighting for months but her body just couldn't take it anymore.

Melissa is there and Teresa and her daughter Gia and our mother passes away in our arms. We're all sobbing and screaming, but there's nothing we can do.

And then it hits us: how are we going to tell Daddy?

I've done a lot of hard things in my life, from playing football to dropping out of college to launching my own business to breaking my engagements to getting the first apartment building to getting Melissa. My family had been through a lot too – Teresa especially – but I don't think anything was as hard as what we had to do that day.

Teresa, Melissa, Gia and I, we go back to St. Joe's in Wayne, and the minute we walk in the room, my dad just starts yelling, "No!"

He knows why we're all there without us having to say anything. We're trying to explain, we're trying to calm him down, but he has just lost his queen. His cries are like screams.

We all start crying and hugging him. We stayed with him for five or six hours, just trying to calm him down.

We were so lost. We never thought our mom would go first and now she was gone.

But when we lose people we love, we have no choice. We have to put our head down and just keep running.

I go to the funeral home and I pick out this beautiful gold casket. I'd never had to do that before.

We book the funeral and wait for Pop to get out of the hospital. Five days later, he signs himself out. We keep the funeral small. There's like 20 people from our family.

My dad wanted to see my mom. We wheel him in to see her because he's still too weak to walk and he sees her there and just loses it again.

We were all lost. All I could do was cry, but even when people we love die, we still gotta keep going. So we made it through the funeral. We made it through those hard days. I went back to work, and we worked together to take care of my pop.

Teresa and I had practically forgotten the hard times behind us.

We were brother and sister again.

As hard as it all was, I knew that in her own way, my mom had brought us together again.

Because no matter how hard life gets or how bad your heart gets broken, you need the love of your family.

Later, my father told me, "You were her life. You were the one person she ever really cared about."

The thing is, I learned how to love my wife because I watched how much my mom and pop loved each other. My father is a tough man, but the way he held my mother up on a pedestal showed me how to treat a woman.

He showed me what it meant to be a man.

And when my mother died, he showed me how important it is to cherish the people we love when they're alive.

No matter what was happening in our lives or on the show, I knew that I wanted to cherish Melissa. I wanted to put my head down and just keep running.

Because that's the only way to win this game of life.

CHAPTER 14

Stay Humble

No one can prepare you for fame.

Melissa and I had no clue what we were signing up for when we agreed to do *Housewives*.

Melissa thought it would be fun, but I just hoped it wouldn't interfere too much with my work. But our lives are changed forever. And it's not just our lives. It's our kids' lives too.

The thing is, my father is a good man who raised me to be a great man.

He showed me how to work, but he was never really able to show up for me the way I want to for my kids.

All he did was work, and I want to really be there.

Between my wife and my job and the show, the best way for me to stay humble is to focus on being a dad.

I spend a lot of time with my kids. I became their football coach. I go to see my daughter cheerlead.

Melissa and I, as busy as we are, we work really hard to make sure our kids are part of that. We show up to everything they do because when you're a kid and you look out in the audience, you're only looking for your parents.

Your parents are the most important thing in the world to you.

So it doesn't matter that we're on TV or how much money we're making or what kind of car we're driving. If we're not showing up for our kids, we're not really successful.

Because it would be easy to raise spoiled kids who don't know how to work for anything. We watch a lot of other people with money do that.

Melissa and I didn't come from that. We're both just working-class Italians from New Jersey and we don't want to forget that. We don't want our kids to forget that either.

Our kids still do chores. They still have to go to football practice and listen to their coaches. They still have to give 100%. And I tell them, "We have to work twice as hard because of the show." Because people see it, and they've got opinions, and we've got to show them who we really are.

I've watched a lot of people get famous and forget that.

Suddenly, they think they're better than other people. They don't want to hang out with the fans. They think they're some big-time celebrity, and I'm like, "What? You're the same person you were before. What's wrong with you?"

I mean, I get it. Fame goes to your head.

People tell you how great you are, and you start thinking the same thing.

You're like, "Hey, maybe I am too good for this job and for my wife or whatever."

You start walking around all pompous and stuff, but then you see yourself on TV, and you're like, "Who's that asshole?"

I didn't want to see myself like that.

I wanted to stay the same guy I always was.

And I realized the best way to do that was to teach my kids to do the same.

I always tell my daughter that the most important thing she has is her reputation.

I tell her every day: it's like we're walking along the edge of a knife and we can't fall off. You make one mistake, and everyone will know about it.

I tell it to my boys too because, now more than ever, you can't mess up. People will know about it immediately, and anything you do can ruin your life.

Even if it doesn't get all over social media, which for them, happens all the time. People talk to each other.

You could be a real partier in high school and maybe clean your act up, but then you go to get a job and the new boss there, he went to your high school, and he sees your name, and he's like, "That guy is a mess up."

You just never know who is going to remember you.

And when you're on TV, a lot of people are going to remember you.

That's why Melissa, the kids and I, we gotta stay humble.

We gotta stick with the lessons and morals we were raised with.

And those lessons really matter when it comes to business.

Since I started on the show, being humble is the most important thing I do at my work.

Because everyone thinks I'm this rich guy, if I come in acting like it they won't take my business seriously.

They'll think my business is a joke even though I was doing it for years before the show.

There's an Italian saying, "Chi è asino e cervo si crede, al saltar della fossa se n'avvede," which basically means, "if you're a deer pretending you're a stag, you're gonna fall in a ditch."

I gotta be who I am if I want to be successful in business. I can't pretend to be someone else or listen to who other people think I am.

I gotta be me.

Because the minute you forget where you came from, the devil starts winning. He starts telling you lies, and you begin to believe them.

People who watch the show usually come up and hug me. Because they know I'm just an average kid with a shoemaker dad from the hood. And I'm never gonna change.

I get up every day and work all day like a dog, wearing my dirty work boots. Then we go out and we do an appearance with people who treat me like a celebrity.

The next day, I get up and go back to work at 5:00 am.

That's what it's been like for the last eight years of our life.

So much has happened.

My son Joey was born on the show. My mother died.

My sister and I fought and got back together and fought and got back together again.

It's been the same for Melissa and Teresa.

But at the end of the day, the most important thing in our lives isn't the show. It's not our jobs. It's our kids.

They mean everything to us, and even when we start to forget who we are, when we start getting wrapped up in this fame business, they keep us humble.

That's what kids do. They don't care about anything but getting your attention, and they want that more than any toy in the world.

Melissa and I are on the same page about that. We don't care if there are cameras around. We don't care what happens on the show. As long as we respect each other, and show up for our kids, we'll stay humble.

That is what helps keep me successful.

Real estate, relationships, reality shows…it's all the same.

You show people who you really are. You treat them right. You stay humble. You work hard. And you make your dreams come true.

I remember doing landscaping and seeing these guys in these big houses, playing with their kids in the backyard. I wanted to be those guys.

Now I am. I can take care of my family, and I can be there for them.

It doesn't matter whether Melissa is a Real Housewife or if I'm a Real Husband. We're real people. Real people who have made all their dreams come true.

Conclusion

In life, no matter what comes your way, you gotta be strong.

When the economy crashed back in 2008, I watched a lot of guys give up. Some of them killed themselves but most of them just walked out of the business.

They went and got that salaried job with weekly money. They had dreams. They wanted to build things and make things happen, but they gave up.

Look, there's nothing wrong with weekly money. But if you want to be the CEO, you gotta get out and fight to be the CEO.

But not in a nasty way. Because what made me get through the tough times, why I kept my business in 2008 and didn't lose it all is because, at the end of the day, I'm a good person. And being a good person is way more important than being a good businessman.

It's what keeps you going when the times get tough.

It's what helps you become successful.

All my biggest deals, all my successes, and all my wealth has come from being a good person in this life. I would lose a bid on a building to a richer guy offering more money and the owners would come back and say, "We love you, Joe, and we want you to have it."

And at home, being a good person is the only thing that matters. How you treat your girlfriend or boyfriend, your husband or wife, how you treat your mother and your father, your kids and your brother and sister, all of that is what actually makes you successful.

The money and the deals? They'll come and go. But your family, they're all you've really got.

The Italians say, "Chi si volta, e chi si gira, sempre a casa va finire," which means: "No matter where you go or turn, you will always end up at home."

I think that's what Melissa and Teresa and myself have all learned from *The Real Housewives of New Jersey*. No matter where we go, no matter what red carpet or TV show we're on or magazine we're in, the only thing that matters is that we end up at home.

I guess that's why I love building real estate so much. Because you're giving people homes. You're reminding them of family, and you're helping to build something from nothing.

Just like I did.

And none of that happens without a lot of hard work.

You gotta take risks in life, and, yeah, you gotta have balls.

The minute you say, "I can't," you've already lost.

Life is all about winning.

So let's get out there and do this. Let's win the game of the life. Because that's the Gorga way.

Acknowledgements

To my Pop – As I've been writing this book, I've realized how much you've taught me. Even when your lessons were hard, and you pounded them into me, you helped make me the man I am today. I thank you for being my pop and my role model.

To my mother – I miss you so much. Thank you for giving me your love and support and a home-cooked meal no matter what I did – or how late I came home.

Melissa – I fell in love with you the moment I put my eyes on you. You've made my life complete, and your honesty, faith, and support in all my crazy ventures have helped make me successful. You're the best thing that ever happened to me, and I can't wait to grow old with you and hold our grandchildren in our arms. I love you, babe.

To Antonia, Gino, and Joey – You are everything I ever wanted in life. You are the reason I get up and fight every day so you don't have to. Your daddy will be by your side for the rest of your lives. God couldn't have given us better kids. The three of you are the best there is.

To Teresa – You were always the one who trusted me and supported me. From letting me max out your cards for my first business to today, you've been my best friend and my sister. If I could change the last few years for you, I would, but I also know our Mommy and Daddy made us strong so we can overcome anything. I know you will. And I'll be here for you.

To my amazing Marco family, and especially Donna Marco, my wonderful mother in law – Thank you for being my second family. You have helped me through the hard times and have been such an amazing part of my life. I am grateful for you every day, and I love you all very much.

To my best friend Bobby Schetelich – Since the day I met you, you've been my best friend, and you've been in my corner ever since. I love you, brother.

Kenneth O'Neil and Frank Weber – Thank you for believing in me and getting me the loans that started it all. You've helped me get to where I am today.

Jerome Sahlman – You've been a father figure and an amazing friend to me. Thank you for helping me through the hard times in life and for supporting me over the years.

Anna David – Thank you for making this book happen – you're amazing! You know what you're doing and I'm excited I've gotten to be a part of Light Hustle.

Kristen McGuiness – You truly inspire me. You did this book between moving and having a baby, and I can't thank you enough for helping me tell my story. You're a hustler and I love it!

Thank you to Darren Prince for pushing me to do this book and to Jules Feiler for helping me get the word out about it.

To the Bravo family, Sirens Media, and Andy Cohen – Thank you for all opportunities. You've become a second family, and I've grown with you over the years, through the good times and the bad.

And last but not least, thank you God for opening all these windows even after the doors have closed. As Melissa says, "Thank you, Jesus."

Made in the USA
San Bernardino, CA
10 December 2019